"As the world lurches from one crisis to another on a long-term trajectory of disaster, we find ourselves in need of new ideas that are not just thought-provoking but action-promoting. Hosseini and Gills' *Capital Redefined* seeks to meet that need. In six concise chapters they invite us to reimagine theory of value from a commonist perspective in an age of climate and ecological emergency. The book is a welcome first step and should be essential reading in post-capitalist critical theory."

Jamie Morgan, *Professor of Economics, co-edits* Real World Economics Review, *and co-author of* Post Neo-liberal Economics

"Many current proposals for emancipatory alternatives center around the notion of commons and experiences of commoning. In their book, "Capital Redefined," Hosseini and Gills present a compelling and consistent argument that places "true value" at the core of the defetishization of capitalism. Their commonist value theory enhances the socio-economic functioning of a more desirable and alternative world. The book will undoubtedly shape the debate about radical political strategies."

Ulrich Brand, *Professor of International Politics, University of Vienna, Austria, and co-author of* Imperial Mode of Living. Everyday Life and the Ecological Crisis of Capitalism

"A thought-provoking theoretical exploration that forces us to critically reflect on how we frame our conceptual views and carry out political actions. A tour de force, it provides original and fresh perspectives on how we think, or ought to think, of contemporary global burning issues such as the politics of and the struggles for land and food in the context of production and social reproduction."

Saturnino M. Borras Jr., *co-editor of* The Oxford Handbook of Land Politics

"If you want to get serious with the Marxian debates concerning the labor theory of value—and everything that surrounds it—then this book is a must read!"

Alexander Dunlap, *Visiting Research Fellow, Global Development Studies, University of Helsinki, Finland*

"S.A. Hamed Hosseini and Barry K. Gills in their Capital Redefined have made a significant contribution to the ongoing debate surrounding the political economy of capitalism and the quest for alternative economic principles. In their book, they delve into the limitations of Marxist value theory while exploring its potential in shaping post-capitalist development, expand the focus beyond the production of commodity value to include the realization of a more-than-human (commonist) approach to value-setting, offering insights that contribute to a new political economy and a society prioritizing the well-being of humanity and the environment. This thought-provoking book adds depth and insight to the discourse, making it an essential read for those interested in exploring new avenues for socio-economic transformation."

Boris Y Kagarlitsky, professor of Moscow Higher School for Social and Economic Sciences, editor of "Rabkor"' web-journal, author of *Between Class and Discourse: Left Intellectuals in Defence of Capitalism* (2020).

Capital Redefined

Capital Redefined presents a unique perspective on the nature of "capital," departing from the prevailing reductionist accounts. Hosseini and Gills offer an expanded perspective on Marxian value theory by addressing its main limitations and building their own integrative value theory. They argue that the current understanding of "value" must be re-examined and liberated from its subservient ties to capital while acknowledging the ways in which capital appropriates value. This is achieved by differentiating between "fetish value" created by capital and "true value" generated through various commons-based forms of coexistence.

The authors propose a defetishization of value by rejecting the commonly accepted idea of its objectivity. They introduce their "commonist value theory," which redefines capital as both the product and process of perverting the fundamental commoning causes of true value into sources of fetish value. Capital is theorized through a "modular" framework, where multiple intersecting processes constitute a comprehensive power structure, a "value regime," representing an unprecedented degree of the domination of capital over life. Their theory reconciles two apparently incompatible views on the notion of value. One view encompasses all inputs involved in capitalist value production and conflates intrinsic and commodity values. The other warns against this conflation as it treats capital as an entity tightly associated only with commodity production and wage labor.

The authors believe that establishing alternative forms of value creation based on normative principles of living in commons is crucial as an analytical base for criticizing existing power structures and economic systems. The book offers a theoretical foundation for transforming our life worlds toward "post-capitalist" futures. It appeals to scholars and students in various fields, such as political economy, capitalism, and post-capitalist studies, economic and political sociology, globalization, development studies, social ecology, and ecological philosophy.

S. A. Hamed Hosseini is Senior Lecturer in Sociology at the College of Human and Social Futures, University of Newcastle (UON), Australia. He is a fellow of the World Academy of Art and Science, founder, and director of UON Alternative Futures Research Network, founder, and editor of "Common Alternatives" initiative (www.thecommonalts.com), co-founder and convenor of Alternative Futures Research Hub (UON's first community-partnered research hub), and co-founder and co-director of the New Economy Network Australia Research Hub.

Barry K. Gills is Professor of Global Development Studies at the University of Helsinki, Finland, and co-founder and active member of the Extractivisms and Alternatives Initiative (ExAlt) based at the university (www.exalt.fi). He is Editor-in-Chief of the journal *Globalizations* and a fellow of the World Academy of Art and Science.

Rethinking Globalizations

Edited by **Barry K. Gills**, *University of Helsinki, Finland* and **Kevin Gray**, *University of Sussex, UK.*

This series is designed to break new ground in the literature on globalization and its academic and popular understanding. Rather than perpetuating or simply reacting to the economic understanding of globalization, this series seeks to capture the term and broaden its meaning to encompass a wide range of issues and disciplines and convey a sense of alternative possibilities for the future.

Challenging Authoritarian Capitalism
The Transformative Power of the World Social Forum
Edited by Thomas Wallgren, Uddhab Pd. Pyakurel, Catalina Revollo Pardo and Teivo Teivainen

The Reconfiguration of Twenty-first Century Latin American Regionalism
Actors, Processes, Contradictions and Prospects
Edited by Rowan Lubbock and Ernesto Vivares

Capitalism, Coronavirus and War
A Geopolitical Economy
Radhika Desai

The Rise of Green Extractivism
Extractivism, Rural Livelihoods and Accumulation in a Climate-Smart World
Natacha Bruna

Globalization, Urbanization, and Civil Society
A Non-Western Critique
Bagoes Wiryomartono

Capital Redefined
A Commonist Value Theory for Liberating Life
S. A. Hamed Hosseini and Barry K. Gills

For more information about this series, please visit: https://www.routledge
.com/Rethinking-Globalizations/book-series/RG

Capital Redefined

A Commonist Value Theory for Liberating Life

S. A. Hamed Hosseini and Barry K. Gills

Routledge
Taylor & Francis Group
LONDON AND NEW YORK

First published 2024
by Routledge
4 Park Square, Milton Park, Abingdon, Oxon OX14 4RN

and by Routledge
605 Third Avenue, New York, NY 10158

Routledge is an imprint of the Taylor & Francis Group, an informa business

© 2024 S. A. Hamed Hosseini and Barry K. Gills

The right of S. A. Hamed Hosseini and Barry K. Gills to be identified as authors of this work has been asserted in accordance with sections 77 and 78 of the Copyright, Designs and Patents Act 1988.

Funded by the University of Helsinki, Finland, and the University of Newcastle, Australia.

Trademark notice: Product or corporate names may be trademarks or registered trademarks, and are used only for identification and explanation without intent to infringe.

British Library Cataloguing-in-Publication Data
A catalogue record for this book is available from the British Library

Library of Congress Cataloging-in-Publication Data
Names: Hosseini, S. A. Hamed, author. | Gills, Barry K., 1956- author.
Title: Capital redefined: a commonist value theory for liberating life /
S.A. Hamed Hosseini and Barry K. Gills.
Description: Abingdon, Oxon; New York, NY: Routledge, 2024. | Series:
Rethinking globalizations | Includes bibliographical references and index.
Identifiers: LCCN 2023028542 (print) | LCCN 2023028543 (ebook) |
ISBN 9781032374765 (hardback) | ISBN 9781032374772 (paperback) |
ISBN 9781003340386 (ebook)
Subjects: LCSH: Capital. | Value.
Classification: LCC HB501 .H85 2024 (print) | LCC HB501 (ebook) |
DDC 330.12/2–dc23/eng/20230825
LC record available at https://lccn.loc.gov/2023028542
LC ebook record available at https://lccn.loc.gov/2023028543

ISBN: 978-1-032-37476-5 (hbk)
ISBN: 978-1-032-37477-2 (pbk)
ISBN: 978-1-003-34038-6 (ebk)

DOI: 10.4324/9781003340386

Typeset in Times New Roman
by Deanta Global Publishing Services, Chennai, India

Contents

Acknowledgments

We gratefully acknowledge the University of Newcastle and the University of Helsinki for their contributions to the production costs of this book as an Open Access resource. We would also like to thank the three anonymous reviewers of the book proposal for their valuable feedback, Dr. Elizabeth Adamczyk for her assistance with proofreading the initial draft, Ms. Hannah Rich, Ms. Helen Birchall and their teams at Routledge Publishing.

Preface

The current era is characterized by the pervasive dominance of capital, with its presence and power extending to every aspect of social life. The influence of capital has reached unprecedented heights, presenting a potentially perilous situation. It is well-known that capital controls economic activity, with corporations and affluent individuals wielding vast pecuniary resources and having enormous sway over financial markets, business decisions, and government policies. The insatiable greed and profit-seeking of corporations have resulted in an alarming concentration of wealth and power, leading to staggering levels of inequality and detrimental effects on health, education, and social mobility. Additionally, the all-encompassing grip of capitalism has inflicted severe ecological devastation, with carbon emissions, pollution, and biodiversity loss irreparably damaging the cycles of life and causing ecosystems to collapse (Panayotakis *et al.*, 2021; Desai, 2023). All of this is occurring amid intensifying global economic competition and geopolitical tensions between established and emerging poles within the world capitalist system.

The fundamental drive of capital, the relentless pursuit of profit, paradoxically endangers its own ecological foundations while also opening new pathways for growth and expansion. Capital has become untamable within the necessary timeframe and scale imposed by the laws of nature, for example, in the field of Earth System Science (Armstrong McKay *et al.*, 2022). The necessity of addressing the global ecological crises at their roots through radical structural changes has never been so imperative, and yet evidently impossible within the present structures of the dominance of capital.

Capitalism, as a socio-ecological formation with a global reach, inherently lacks the capacity to unite various actors, such as governments, businesses, and communities, to effectively address the worldwide existential threat of climate change driven by the expansion of capital. The post-Cold War order, allegedly built upon the 'golden arches of peace,' is on the brink of another historical phase of escalating international conflicts, consisting of a combined geoeconomic and geostrategic rivalry between competing capitalist states and blocs in the context of an increasingly multipolar world order (Chomsky and Prashad, 2022). The realm of capital's dominion now includes not only the sphere of physical commodity production but every other domain of societal living where the so-called 'value' can be extracted, appropriated, and accumulated.

As the rich continue to amass capital, the penchant for funnelling funds into financial and extractive pursuits rather than into productive and communal goals has paved the way for a surge in financialized capital, exacerbating already-widespread global disparities. The vast accumulation of financial and non-financial assets worldwide, surpassing 530 trillion US dollars and amounting to over 650% of global GDP by the end of 2021 (Zakrzewski *et al.*, 2022), is predominantly controlled by a select few who prioritize investing in lucrative and rent-seeking endeavors over ventures that may have greater social benefits but are deemed less profitable. This widespread trend has gained significant traction since the economic upheaval of 2008 (Hudson, 2015), further perpetuating the deep-seated inequities of our global economic landscape.

Most contemporary economic systems are profoundly influenced by the paradoxical idea of the 'infinite growth' of capital in the context of finite resources, whose intrinsic values are replaced with exchange values, prices, and profit margins. The pursuit of profit-driven 'value' production under the dominance of 'capital' has resulted in and will continue to lead to socially and ecologically unsustainable futures. Additionally, the rapid growth of artificial intelligence and industrial innovations disconnected from the intrinsic needs of societies and contemporary ecological imperatives further exacerbate these challenges.

The coming decades will be an era of increasingly militant and radicalized resurgences, entailing multiple social instabilities and intensifying social conflicts within and between states. This will entail encounters and rivalry between the strategies of *alternative forms of capital* and *alternatives to capital*. Polarization, mobilization, and contestation between these increasingly radicalized antipodal visions will shape the future of human social order and our species' relationship with the planet. In our view, these characteristics are set to define the twenty-first century, and the outcome will determine the fate of all life on earth.

As we have argued in previous works, the global primacy of capital has reached an unprecedented and pivotal point in its history, which has serious implications for critical theory (Hosseini, 2020; Hosseini and Gills, 2020b; Hosseini and Gills, 2020a; Hosseini *et al.*, 2020; Hosseini *et al.*, 2022). Although the desire to understand capital has animated debates for the past two and a half centuries, its dynamics have been constantly changing, making it a complex and evolving system with significant flexibility and resilience over time and across different regions. Consequently, there remain unresolved debates and disagreements among scholars regarding the nature of capital. Given the pressing need for a genuinely sustainable and equitable future, it is crucial that we engage in introspective discussions about the essence of capital to reshape the frameworks that underpin our understanding of how capital comes into being and functions. As we will argue in the first chapter, *it is now necessary to redefine capital through a transformative theorization of value, 'beyond capital,' to build a new reality that better serves humanity and works towards enhancing and preserving all life on Earth for the future.*

The global financial crisis of 2008 was a turning point after which 'the C word' (capital/capitalism) found its way back to the center of critical social imagination and debate over the nature of capital. A shift in the political consciousness of these social forces is rapidly becoming a focal point in critical scholarly discourses that increasingly examine the systemic roots of the imminent socio-ecological calamities facing us during the twenty-first century. And this has resulted in a surge of attention to Marx's legacy. An effective redefinition of capital is impossible without a sincere engagement with the seminal ideas and enduring legacy of Karl Marx and Friedrich Engels.

The groundbreaking contribution of Karl Marx to the theorization of capital and his insightful perspectives on the 'logic' of the historical expansion of capital, its inherent 'contradictions,' and 'crisis tendencies' are profoundly important. Marx's legacy remains sufficiently powerful to be a point of departure or reference for every new serious debate on this issue. His theory of capital, since its inception, has served as a platform not only for later Marxist orthodoxies but also for numerous revisionists, reformists, and antagonists of his approach, interpretations, and prescriptions. However, alongside the recent revitalization of system-oriented transformative consciousness, some archaic lines of controversies around the nature and future of capital and capitalism, between different factions of the 'old Left,' including Marxist subdivisions, continue to influence emerging debates and their associated practices of action.

The effort to reunite critical theory with its Marxist roots in a dynamic way faces significant intellectual challenges. The emergence of poststructuralist, pluriversalist, and postmodernist criticisms of modernity and universalism has complicated the relationship between critical theory and Marxist value theory. In the second half of the twentieth century, some critical theorists challenged the limits of traditional Marxist analyses of labor, value, and class struggle and explored alternative frameworks that prioritize issues such as culture, identity, power, and discourse, leading to a distancing of critical theory from Marxist value theory.

The predominance of culturalism and post-modernism in critical social theory has transformed the general academic mindset in the global North. This tendency has been reinforced by the decline of collectivized labor in centralized mass production, the ascendancy of post-Fordist decentralized production, and the middle classes' extended capacity to maintain their standard of living by working longer hours, importing cheap goods made from cheap natural resources produced by cheap labor, often in the global South, and the massive expansion of credit and finance systems facilitating significant personal and commercial debt.

Although the rise of high-tech has brought about the decentralization of capitalist production relations and the acceleration of information circulation, it has not spelled the end of monopoly capitalism; instead, it has morphed into a more sophisticated and lethal version. The post-pandemic era is revealing a paradigm shift in the world's capitalist system, where the organized life, or 'life-domain,' is facing an unprecedented existential threat, as the window to save the planet rapidly closes, highlighting the intrinsic value of life above all else. The impending apocalypse is acutely felt at the grassroots level, as evidenced by numerous recent movements representing a new generation of revolutionary tendencies that we call 'Revolutions for Life' or 'Life Revolts', led by subalterns who courageously risk their lives to defend the most precious and endangered entity: *life* itself.

All of this requires transformative social theory to catch up with the new unfolding of human conscience; an overdue 'axiological turn' requiring the centering of the *imperative normativity of life* in our critical ontological encounters with reality. The axiological turn is about giving primacy to the 'true value' that emanates from life and nourishes life. *The true sources of value are all in commons form.* Life itself is a commons, perhaps the most fundamental of them all after the cosmos. Life is a unity emerging out of a web of diversity. It is dynamic and in constant motion, cyclical yet self-enduring and self-flourishing, if its boundaries are not transgressed and if its capacities to thrive are not undermined, especially ironically in the name of 'value'!

This book proposes a novel approach to theorizing capital and 'capitalism' by incorporating the 'normativity of life' into its critical analysis and recognizing the absence of inherent true value in capital. It challenges the prevailing belief that capital is the ultimate source of worth and redirects our attention to the flourishing of life and the preservation and enhancement of its thriving capacities. This transformative perspective calls for a fundamental re-evaluation of our socio-economic and political systems, aiming to transcend the destructive contradictions and deficiencies of capitalism.

Redefining capital necessitates redefining 'value' in the process. Although the notion of value has been neglected in most modern social theories (Pitts, 2021), Marx's assertion that "value forms the foundation of capital" (Marx, 1993: 421) remains as relevant as ever. This, however, raises the question of how to redefine capital while also acknowledging the value of socio-ecological relations in shaping it. These relations should not be seen simply as a context or precondition, but rather as a set of interrelated causal mechanisms that are embedded *in* and *against* capital. Merely contemplating the socio-ecological, cultural, and (geo-)political dimensions of capitalist functionality as the vital conditions for economic exploitation, without theorizing their re/construction in the process of capitalist value production, is inadequate to grasp the complex challenges posed by capital, and the prospects for profound conflicts and paradigm shifts.

Redefining capital and value entails revisiting and expanding upon Marxian conceptions while deploying a new perspective inspired by a new discourse on the 'commons' and 'commoning' developed here in the form of a 'modular conceptual framework.' *This framework, built on a critical realist ontology, conceptualizes capital as an ensemble of multiple interrelated socio-historical (infra)processes, rather than as an analytically isolated inner structure of 'the capitalist system'* (see Chapters 3 and 4). This perspective goes beyond the limitations of productivism, economism, and the post-value turn while emphasizing intersectional and ecological dimensions and complex relationships with post-capitalist alternatives and transformative movements.

This book reflects on the strengths, potentialities, and limitations of the Marxian tradition of understanding capital in terms of value. It then argues for expanding on these limitations and proposes relevant solutions by presenting a new normative value theory that prioritizes the sources of life as commons and their intrinsic value. Thus, offering a *commonist value theory*. This theory encompasses both critical and analytical elements. According to this new theory, the ultimate sources of what we call '*true value*' are precisely the organized life's *condiciones sine quibus non*, which under capitalist relations are perverted into the causal sources of what we call '*fetish value*' as the essence of capital (Hosseini, 2022a).

True value is *sustainably* (re)produced *only* through the commoning modes of living and interconnecting. A commons, whether material or immaterial, naturally occurring or manufactured, is a living organism made up of communities of interconnected and interdependent entities. In normal conditions, the activities of these entities borrow their vitality from the entirety of the commons and, in return, contribute to the survival and thriving of the whole, inclusive of all individual (living) entities. *One for all, all for one, and unity in diversity* – this is how true value is regenerated.

Under the supremacy of capital, however, the so-called modern civilization emerged as a development through which not only were commons expropriated, but also de-commonized, losing their essence as commons. Capitalism has now become *capitality*, a life-killing mode deeply coded into the genetics of our daily lives, thanks to its axiological primacy. *Only a profound (re-) commonization of our modern socio-ecological relations can liberate life from the immense grip and power of capital; a transformative process that holds the potential to effectively transcend the predicament of mere survival, while also transforming ubiquitous capitalist relations.*

1 Introduction

On the Necessity of Liberating Value from Capital[1]

At the heart of our intellectual journey in this book lies the profound realization that in order to redefine capital, we must first engage in a transformative discourse that places (redefining) value at its very core. In the face of an imminent convergence of ecological and social crises, it becomes increasingly evident that the immense influence wielded by capital is at the core of these threatening upheavals, jeopardizing the future stability and well-being of (extra-)humanity. To navigate the treacherous waters of the present crises, we must acknowledge that the redefinition of capital necessitates a profound reassessment of its very foundation. Value, as the driving force behind capital, holds the key to unlocking new possibilities and transforming our understanding of economic and social systems. By critically examining the concept of value in a capitalist social formation, we gain insight into the processes and mechanisms by which capital exerts its power and influence. By gaining this insight, we can identify the limitations and negative consequences of the current model and seek alternative approaches that prioritize (extra) human well-living and genuine ecological sustainability. The re-evaluation of value is a crucial step in challenging the dominant capitalist paradigm and envisioning alternative models of social and economic organization.

To begin our argument: if we accept the proposition that any quality necessary or advantageous for the survival and self-fulfillment of organized life (human and non-human) is of undeniable 'value' and if we consider capitalism as a socio-ecological formation under which all the ultimate sources of this '*true value*' are now at stake, it would then become imperative to retheorize 'value' and its ultimate sources, not only to reflect this dire reality but also to manifest the potential for real human liberation. The ultimate sources of 'true value' have been depleted regarding their capacities to sustain life: 'Mother nature' (as the commoning source of *liveability*) is seriously ill, and 'labor' (as a re/productive, creative, and life-enhancing commons) is typically overexploited, alienated, and/or made superfluous, while 'communal solidarity and convivial coexistence' are severely damaged. Global 'high-tech' and information technology complexes now exist to confuse and distract the masses (using highly sophisticated 'weapons of mass distraction'), conditioning people to behave through their swelling sense of resentment, fear, and

DOI: 10.4324/9781003340386-1

even hatred of the Other. Meanwhile, while emancipatory movements strive to harness their prefigurative potential, they frequently encounter substantial structural barriers both internally and externally, hindering their ability to fully actualize their goals.

Key historical processes that generate crises include the hyper-exploitation of labor and of the environment, underinvestment in necessary infrastructure, paired with over-concentration of wealth, capital, and power. *Parasitic accumulation* is a defining feature of the conditions outlined above, and it provokes acute systemic crises. All are present to a high degree in today's world system, and we are indeed in a general world system crisis. *The reality of capital delegitimizes any analytically objective perception of 'value under capital' as (true) 'value.'* Therefore, a fundamentally new line of theorization is needed, where value is defined from a more-than-human societal perspective, within a normative frame of reference. This new notion of value, referred to as true value, is based on *the negation of capital, understood as a life-negating value in operation, i.e., a fetish (value) sold to us as (true) value* (Hosseini, 2022a).

This necessary retheorization of value will have significant implications for our relationship with capital and capitalism. It is time to move beyond the acceptance of *the notion of value as dictated by capital.*[2] It is time to differentiate between 'fetish value' (functioning as negative value in society) and 'true value,' the former being the product of capital and the latter being capital's prey but also its antidote. This, we believe, is a matter of historical necessity in our theoretical praxis (action-oriented theorization as part of our historical praxis).

In this book, we introduce the term 'fetish value' to distinguish our conception of value from that of classical political economy and its Marxian critique, encompassing Marx's idea of (commodity) value but extending beyond it, as we will elaborate. Fetish value should not be confused with Marx's 'fictitious value' that refers to 'fictitious capital' as its embodiment versus 'real value' embodied in productive capital. While keeping the notion of value within the contours of production relations, David Harvey instead prefers the notion of 'anti-value' (Harvey, 2018b).[3] To avoid confusion, we have chosen to use the terms 'fetish value' (not to be confused with Baudrillard's concept either) and 'true value' instead (see Chapter 2).

The history of capitalism has been tightly associated with the history of colonialism (-imperialism) and (European/Western) Enlightenment-induced modernity. Their coexistence has certainly not been a coincidence. The three have functioned interdependently, yet, relatively autonomously, and thus, the latter two (colonialism and Western modernity) could theoretically continue to exist and contribute to a downward spiral of the decline of modern civilization even in the absence of the dominance of capital (as arguably they did under the Fascist and Communist states of the twentieth century). Perhaps it is this historical association, however, that has resulted in the mutation of each of them in recent centuries, morphing into modern phenomena with essential differences compared to their primordial (or 'precapitalist') historical forms. And yet, in our view, it is the nature of this association that has received the least amount of theoretical effort. Regrettably, this book is not about theorizing the triad association, and for a good reason. To make the theorization of this association possible, first, we need to redefine capital since the existing notions can hardly be related to colonialism and modernity beyond simple descriptions of their historical coexistence. The focus of this book is thus on redefining capital and capitalism in order to meet the aforementioned prerequisite initially.

Colonialism and modernity each have their own embedded mechanisms, which have already been the subjects of meticulous critical investigation, and theorization, over the past century; mechanisms like rationalizing, instrumentalizing, standardizing, anthropomorphizing, classifying, codifying, and universalizing under the modernist paradigm, and mechanisms such as extracting, confiscating, occupying, dispossessing, enclosing, patenting, exploiting, subjugating, orientalizing, de-identifying, enslaving, and creating relations of dependency under the colonialist–imperialist paradigm (premodern, modern, or postmodern). Not all these mechanisms can be brought into a single theory within the scope of this book. *Our goal is mostly to outline the principles of a new framework that can be later extended further through future argumentations by incorporating as many mechanisms as possible into more detailed and synthesized analyses.*

In recent decades, critical theorists have made numerous attempts to move beyond the traditional understanding of capital as a 'social process' in which money generates more money by extracting the 'surplus value' produced within capitalist commodity production relations. In the conventional Marxian framework, capital is indeed theorized as a 'societal process' through which surplus value (in both real and fictitious forms) is produced and controlled via 'unsustainable' and 'un-sovereign' ways of exploiting labor (both manual and intellectual) as the ultimate source of (commodity) value. Land (in the form of landed properties), 'reproductive labor' (which is essential for the reproduction of labor), and 'nature' (which provides 'free gifts' such as energy sources, mineral resources, the atmosphere, the earth's bio-capacity, fertile soil, water, etc.) are all considered to be necessary conditions for wage labor.

A growing number of revisionist voices which have not abandoned value theory have already been arguing for widening the notion of value to include uncommodified forms of labor/work. They normally forget, however, that value in Marx's *Capital* is *capitalist (commodity) value*. Thus, the work of nature, the subaltern, communities, and the life-makers can only be validly analyzed if our value theory differentiates between their value when they are outside and inside capitalist production and exchange relations. The challenge at hand is to address the ambiguity that arises from adhering to the Marxian labor theory of commodity value while simultaneously broadening the definition of value under capital to include the intrinsic value of uncommodified qualities (Foster & Burkett, 2018).

Four points are worth mentioning here:

(1) *The polarity between labor and nature/ecology* is one of the significant contradictions of capital. Labor, in its 'natural form,' when considered outside the confines of capitalist social structures, is a manifestation of humanity's innate creative potential, a faculty that has evolved naturally but has been 'abstracted' and profoundly alienated from its natural context by capitalism. In this book, we will argue that this dualism needs to be resolved at the normative level since the two (when unalienated) are not only ontologically entwined but must also restore their lost integration to allow a meaningful transition beyond capital. However, we do not suggest equating or hybridizing the two in our critical 'analyses' of capital, as their effects on capitalist value are distinct. We will explore these effects in more detail later in Chapters 5 and 6.

(2) *We need to differentiate between 'labor' and 'creative power'* (or the 'humans' capacity to be creative') beyond producing the necessary means of subsistence. Work is one of the socially natural forms of humans' creative power that is reified into 'labor' and, thereby, commodity and value forms (made abstract and homogeneous) under the capitalist mode of production, as Marx's value theory entails. In this way, we also distance ourselves from productivist interpretations of Marx without marginalizing commodity production (see also Vitale, 2020).

(3) Although *we argue for closely relating the definition of 'true value' to 'well-living,'* i.e., good life, consciously and conscientiously defined by the associations/communities of free commoners (Hosseini, 2018b), the proposition would still be 'crude' as a practical approach if we consider achieving the communal good life as an ultimate goal, i.e., as an end in itself, while ignoring the necessity of what Marx terms as the "transcendence of human self-estrangement" (Marx et al., 1988, p. 102) as well as what we may call 'existential liberation,' that is, 'exploring and living up to the purpose of Existence.'

(4) Although we may occasionally, loosely, and interchangeably use terms like 'organized life,' 'lifeworld(s),' 'earth system,' and 'web of life,' we are mindful of their specific disciplinary and theoretical connotations, which may limit their compatibilities with our critical social theory. Therefore, we introduce the concept of 'life-domain' *as the interconnected system of all living things and their environment on planet Earth. Life-domain encompasses the biosphere, atmosphere, hydrosphere, and lithosphere and includes all forms of life, from microorganisms to plants and animals. The concept of life-domain emphasizes the interconnectedness and interdependence of all living things and highlights the importance of maintaining the health and balance of the natural world for the well-being of (more than) human societies and future generations.* The life-domain includes human social systems and cultural practices that

shape and are shaped by the living world. It is a holistic domain that encompasses all domains of life, including social, economic, and ecological dimensions of (more-than-human) life, without ignoring their relative autonomy. The use of the word 'domain' is intended to imply both control and power relations but also responsibility and stewardship. The life-domain, unlike the web of life and the like, is more inclusive of the sociology and anthropology of conflictual power relations.[4]

These four points will be incorporated into our arguments throughout the rest of the book.

And so, we pose the question, what analysis of capital will we end up with if we base our theory on the relationship between a primarily normative notion of value (true value) and a primarily analytical one (fetish value) instead of merely relying on the latter? What implications would this have for both transformative theories of change and transformative and revolutionary praxes? By emphasizing the importance of a normative frame of reference, we can consider not only the economic but also the ethical and political dimensions of value production. This approach allows us to imagine alternative economic systems that prioritize social and environmental well-being over profit maximization. The focus shifts from a purely analytical understanding of capitalism as a social and economic system to a holistic approach that considers the social and ecological implications of different forms of value creation and exchange. This requires a nuanced understanding of how value is created and distributed and how it impacts different social groups and the environment. In terms of transformative and revolutionary praxes, the focus would shift from merely challenging existing power relations and economic structures of capitalism to creating alternative forms of value production and exchange that are based on normative principles of social justice and ecological sustainability. This involves a greater emphasis on the collective creation and distribution of value and a rethinking of traditional notions of ownership and property. Such an approach requires us to perceive *capital as both the product and process of the perversion of the most indispensable types of commons vital for the creation of true value.*

Following an Aristotelian fourfold model of causality (i.e., the *efficient, material, formal,* and *final* causes), we consider four irreducible categories as the 'fundamental commons' that (only when) together cause true value: (1) **Creativity** as the 'efficient' commoning cause of true value, comprising (more than) humans' creative capacities to conscientiously achieve and sustain self-fulfilling levels of collective living in balanced coexistence with the (rest of the) life-domain; (2) **Liveability** as the 'material' commoning cause, consisting of the material and immaterial substances, components and inputs necessary for producing true value. These sources evolve naturally through self-sustaining, restorative, and regenerative practices under shared stewardship and collective decision-making across socio-ecological networks of communal life;

(3) **Conviviality** as the 'formal' commoning cause entailing deep interdependence among (more than) human populations, pluriversality of their modes of living and caring, and their communal solidarity inclusive of non-humans, or in other words, the convivial modes of 'living well together' (well-living, *buen vivir*) through (and despite) frictions, tension, disputes, and diversities; and finally; (4) **Alterity** as the 'final' commoning cause of true value, such as organized prefigurative practices and subjectivities (imaginative, symbolic, proactivist) essential for transcending the dominant hierarchical structures and for actualizing rightful ideals, moralities, dreams, more-than-human liberation, purposeful 'well-living,' and a 'free life.' (Refer to the next chapter for further elaboration on these four essential causes of true value.)

As we will argue in the rest of the book, capital can be seen as 'fetish value in motion and operation'; a form that is 'negative' both in function as a destructive force and in magnitude as it is a loss in true value, necessary for the survival and self-fulfillment of organized life. This approach will avoid ambiguity caused by assigning the term 'value' (which inherently implies normativity) to (unfree) labor under capital. Labor in its natural (*un-reified, free*) form is a social commons of the efficient type since the (individual) capacity for creativity and re/production is a *part* and *product* of historically formed collective coexistences. Ignoring this reality results in *confusing labor (under capital), abstract or concrete, with human creative power.* Therefore, as we will discuss, for the abstraction of labor out of its commoning sources (i.e., abstract labor as a reified social form of creative power susceptible to exploitation), capital has to disconnect/alienate labor from its ecological, communal, and political settings. In the capitalist mode of production, the rest of the 'fundamental commons' are treated as preconditions for the production of fetish value, thus making labor deprived of its access to these now peripheralized or colonized commons.

Recent theoretical advancements, especially those after the 2008 Global Financial Crisis (GFC) and the recent global pandemic, attempt to grasp the new nature(s) and forms of capitalism in the new century. However, these efforts focus on capturing new qualities claimed to be the most distinctive relative to the past (e.g., late, post-Fordist, post-industrial, predatory, disaster, radical, surveillance, platform) and thus *fail to provide a dynamic picture of capital's socio-historical totality and continuity based on an integrative value theory.* Some recent radical theorists have rearticulated capitalist expansion and counter-expansion as a double movement of 'enclosure' versus 'commoning,' a welcomed advancement, but still too ambiguous and metaphorical to overcome its consequent simplifications (McCarthy, 2005; Hardt & Negri, 2009; Sevilla-Buitrago, 2015).

Marxist theories of value focus on the internal workings of capitalist production relations and do not extend Marx's value theory to 'capitalism' as a socio-ecological formation. Consequently, many new theories of capitalism lack a coherent theory of value, despite frequently referencing the works of

Marx and Engels, particularly *Capital*. Marx confirmed in the third volume of *Capital* that his work's scope and purpose are 'only' a presentation of "*the inner organisation of the capitalist mode of production, in its ideal average*" (Marx, 2001, p. 1113, added emphasis). Moreover, Marxian literature often fails to conceive capital's intermingling yet perverting relationships with non- and post-capitalist modes of living. Thus, there remains a wide chasm between the Marxian revivalist value theories and critical social theories of capitalism. A new path toward a more consolidated inquiry with profound praxiological implications is required. We aim to suggest a way of building such a path by providing a new analysis capturing the essence and complexities of capital in our era while attempting to overcome the above chasm in the literature and the inadequacies or limitations of a 'double movement' perspective (enclosure versus commoning).

We begin by acknowledging that Marx took extraordinarily important steps toward theorizing capital from its classical political economy roots, and his general approach as outlined in *Capital* functions as a useful paradigm. However, we argue that even (neo-) Marxian conceptions of capital remain captive to embedded capitalist mentalities propagated through critical modernist academic circles. *Capital's nature is not solely processual but also modular, meaning it involves myriad interrelated social-ecological processes rather than any single one* (i.e., accumulation via production, circulation, and distribution). Multiple theories provide essential, albeit partial, explanations for these multiple processes. However, the multisystemic mechanisms through which these processes interact and 'interface' and their constantly evolving relative positions concerning one another (or what we call 'the architecture of capital') have not been the subject of new integrative theorizations. We argue that such a new theorization opens a path to liberate us from the reductionist understanding of 'capital' and 'capitalism,' and their persisting conceptual residues.

In Chapter 2, we identify four key limitations in traditional Marxian ideas of capital, given the current state of the capitalist world system and the various global crises we face. We also offer potential solutions to overcome these limitations. Each of these limitations has been detected and addressed by a different line of reflexive criticism in critical scholarship. However, interestingly, each one corresponds to an irreducible source of 'true value' (or a fundamental commons) as introduced above. We aim to bring these critical reflections together through our proposed modular framework since all four ultimate sources of true value are closely intertwined, and their interactions require an integrative approach. This integrative approach, which we call the 'commonist framework,' is distinctive in the sense that it attempts to outline a new definition of capital, considering it as '*fetish value regime*,' which makes the development of a more coherent praxeology possible.

In Chapters 3 and 4, we expound on the 'architecture of capital' in the form of ideally constructed modules of (inter/in)dependent social (infra-)processes and (meta-) mechanisms. *Capital is analytically deconstructed into its constituting processes (modules)*, and its evolution is discussed closely in association with alter- and counter-processes, and thus perceived more dynamically rather than as a fixed notion, a singular mode of social relations, or a singular process. Chapter 3, by taking a critical realist perspective, discusses the metatheoretical bases of the model, preparing the ground for Chapter 4 to introduce the commonist modular framework.

Chapter 5 revisits and reconstructs Marxian value theory by drawing on the commonist modular framework. We argue that 'labor' is the result of the decommonization of (more than) human creative power through abstraction and appropriation processes. To clarify, 'real abstraction' in the Marxian tradition refers to the process of extracting and reducing complex social relations to a simple measure of value, such as labor time. We will expand this notion by distinguishing between 'primary' and 'secondary' abstractions. 'Primary abstraction' creates labor and labor power outside capitalist production relations, while 'secondary abstraction' results in abstract labor and productive capitalist value represented by exchange value and surplus value. By delineating the two types of real abstraction, we offer potential solutions to disagreements over the suitability of Marxian value theory in the context of post-industrial capitalism.

Chapter 6, drawing on the commonist modular framework, examines recent debates around the capacity of Marxian labor theory of value (LTV) in adequately theorizing affective work, automation, and the ecological profile of capital. The chapter provides an overview of these major debates and discusses how the commonist perception of value can help overcome some of the underlying confusion.

Two important disclaimers are needed in this regard. Firstly, the book's use of the term 'value theory' or 'theory of value' should be interpreted as *a preliminary discussion of a new approach to theorizing capital and counter-capital by re-centering 'value.' The aim is not to present a fully sophisticated metaphysical argument or develop a theoretical framework for a specific empirical research project. Rather than aiming for conclusive arguments, this concise book, serving as the inaugural edition of the first volume in a series, functions as an open invitation to engage in a discussion of its ideas and further develop them into a comprehensive general theory that can be adapted into context-specific middle-range theories. As such, the arguments put forth are intended to be indicative rather than definitive.*

Secondly, the book does not call for a shift from a critical–analytical approach to value to a purely normative one in critical scholarship. Rather, the new approach involves the incorporation of a normative notion of value (value as 'what ought to be valued' or 'what is naturally valued' in what we call the 'commonist state of living') into our analyses of reality, challenging the definition of value as set by capital. *Without the analysis of what constitutes reality, normativity will be reduced to an imaginary utopia that may, at best, function as a source of motivation.* This resembles what capital makes us believe; that our dreams are only dreams. But the normative is the product of constant dialogue between our dreams and experiences of both injustices and of our realized virtues in the past and present. Surely the normative is always distorted by the value systems manufactured to sustain the status quo. But it is the social experiences of, and reflections on, such value systems that fuel the evolution of the normative. Value systems decide what value is on the ground (e.g., is it material wealth, economic productivity, communal well-being, or spiritual growth?). It is the relentless struggles over and negotiations around making, circulating, and taking 'value' that, in (re)turn, determine changes in value systems.

The proposed new 'normative-analytical' value theory (i.e., a normative-analytical approach to theorization) has the power to liberate our analyses and middle-range theories of capitalist relations from the notional influence of 'capitalist value' by identifying four essential commoning causes of true value. By introducing the concept of 'true value,' the normative element of the theory becomes explicit. The theory reconceptualizes capitalist value as 'fetish value.' This form of value is characterized as 'negative' because it serves as a destructive force and represents a loss in true value, rather than being a virtue or a purely analytical construct like exchange value, which carries implicit normative implications. We need to emphasize here that the normative is not baseless in reality, and the analytical is not delusion free. *True value and fetish value do not belong to two essentially different universes,* one being the world of ideals and the other being the world of the real. *Fetish value is a perverted and distorted version of true value.* The fact that true value is not fully 'actualized' does not make it unrealistic and the fact that fetish value is 'actualized' under capital does not make it a reflection of true 'reality.'

Notes

1 This chapter draws on material from the paper titled *Capital as 'Fetish Value' Has No 'True Value'* by Hosseini (2022a).
2 Both classical bourgeois political economy and the Marxian value theory presume this definition.
3 According to Harvey (2018b, pp. 76–77), technical glitches and delays in the circulation of capital give rise to an "anti-value" that transforms into political resistance against commodification and privatization, thus creating an active space for anti-capitalist struggle. Harvey also claims that the working class, however defined, represents the embodiment of anti-value.
4 By including the social and economic systems, as well as the idea of power and resource distribution, the definition acknowledges the role of class conflict and other social inequalities in shaping the relationship between humans and the natural world. Additionally, one could emphasize the importance of social and environmental justice in any discussion of the life-domain to further highlight the need to address issues of inequality and exploitation in our relationship with the rest of nature.

2 Beyond *Capital*

Away from Marx with Marx[1]

We have so far argued for a transformative approach to understanding 'capital as a value regime' that not only creates, circulates, and distributes value (often in a conflictual fashion) but fundamentally defines it as a normative quality to be placed primarily as the 'final cause' of major human activities. As we will discuss in this chapter, classical and Marxian value-based theories of capital have traditionally focused on the former aspect of capital's value regime, taking a critical–analytical stance. However, in recent decades, intellectual and social struggles have shifted toward disputing what should be valued under or beyond the system, and calls for restructuring or replacing the value regime of capital have gained momentum. By returning to the centrality of value in our redefinition of capital today, we may be better equipped to address these pressing demands.

The New Left of the 1960s–1970s, preoccupied with valuing identity, recognition, and culture, gradually gave way to the new 'New Left' of the 1990s–2000s, now more concerned with global injustices and existential threats to life while maintaining concerns with post-material values. A new generation of progressive social and mass movements emerged that, unlike past generations (the so-called Old and the New), tended to be more 'accommodative' and 'transversal,' though less coherently, with potentialities for integration of material/redistributive and post-material/recognitive concerns (Hosseini, 2011, 2013, 2015). On the other hand, (post-/neo-)Marxist, (post-/neo-)anarchist, and (post-/neo)Keynesian accounts of structural crises, as an inherent property of capital, have recently enjoyed a moderate revival (Albritton et al., 2004).

The post-GFC renewed interest in capital and Marx, prompting a crucial inquiry: is there a valid reason to revisit the classical Marxian notion of capital and its linked value theory?[2] We propose that by reinvigorating our engagement with value theory and embracing a fresh conceptualization of value, we can develop a comprehensive framework that incorporates recent critical advancements in counter-system movements and revisionist scholarship.

Most of this chapter offers a critical reflection on the Marxian value-based conception of capital, asking how such a notion, abandoned by mainstream economists, can help us comprehend the complexity of today's world. We will reflect on the strengths, potentialities, and limitations of the Marxian tradition and argue that its important potentialities can yet be used to transcend

DOI: 10.4324/9781003340386-2

its limitations. We identify four limitations that will be discussed concerning (1) *the sphere of creativity beyond production relations*; (2) *the sphere of liveability or vitality*; (3) *the sphere of convivial solidarity and care*; and (4) *the sphere of post-capitalist modes of alterity.* Although Marxist and post-Marxist thinkers have made important attempts to develop and reform the Marxian tradition to address the evolving complexities of capital, we propose that a consolidating effort, centered around the differentiation between true value and fetish value and their ultimate sources, is necessary to overcome these limitations. Our modular integrative framework will be presented in Chapter 4 after presenting its consolidating metatheoretical basis in Chapter 3. This framework reveals how capital as 'fetish value' emerges out of the decommonization of the fundamental causes of 'true value.'

The Dual Character of Value in Theory: The Analytical, the Normative

Although value theories of capital have been largely abandoned in today's social and economic studies, understanding what consists of 'value' for and by society remains an unavoidable underpinning of critical theory. Certainly, the very avoidance of explicit discussions of value does not mean that value theory has become obsolete (Graeber, 2001; De Angelis, 2007; Mazzucato, 2018; Pitts, 2021; Hosseini, 2022a). *Every mode of social living is basically formed and constantly reformed around the ever-changing intersubjective construction and collective realization, distribution, and demolition (or 'negation') of 'value,' in all its possible social-ecological forms, and every social struggle is about controlling and/or liberating such processes.* To reconstruct the infamous maxim by Marx and Engels in the *Communist Manifesto*:

> The history of all hitherto existing societies, and by extension, the henceforth ones, is the history of two separate yet overlapping ideal types of struggles: one is between the value makers and value takers within the dominant value regime over the distribution of value, and the other, a more decisive one, over 'what ought to constitute value' and the foundational structure of the value regime itself. While the former may facilitate important progress, it is the latter that plays a critical role in creating meaningful transformations.
>
> (Hosseini, 2022a, pp. 2–3)

It remains crucial, in the present day as much as it was during the eighteenth and nineteenth centuries, to position value theory at the core of transformative scholarship. By doing so, we can reconstruct it to comprehend the contemporary connection between capital and value, as well as the historical trajectory of capitalist and counter-capitalist relations and their potential evolution in the future.

There have been two general approaches to 'critically' theorizing value under capital. The first is a primarily analytical approach that presumes 'value' to be an *objective* (material or immaterial) *advantageous quality, extracted out of its resources, to sustain and amplify the ruling social order.* 'Value,' here, is constrained within the realm of political economy as a socio-economic phenomenon. This approach aims to demonstrate how the processes of production, circulation, distribution, and value loss, as perceived through the lens of the dominant system, can lead to both the reproduction and maintenance of the ruling order and the emergence of structural contradictions. These contradictions may, in turn, give rise to crises and lead to transformative metabolic shifts. Although primarily analytical and educational in nature, the approach initially presented by Marx in *Capital* holds indirect normative implications as it highlights the exploitation and alienation of the 'value makers,' resulting from the process of value extraction by the 'value takers' (Smetona, 2015). In other words, it is substantially analytical but normative only by implication.

For the critical theory to be transformative, as evident in Marx's general approach, it needs to be as normative–analytical and ontologically integrative as it is praxiologically diversifying. It needs to be based on not only the dialectics between theoretical abstraction and concrete reality but also the dialectics between *reality* (as it happens) and *truth* (reality as it ought to be – morally acceptable and practically prefigurable). As we have argued elsewhere, "to be radically transformative, the critical ought to be morally judgmental" (Hosseini & Gills, 2020b, p. 18). If "the point is to change the world" (Marx & Engels, 1998), then the theorization of reality needs to engage with, rather than isolate itself from, the action-guiding *normativity* embedded in the existing potentialities for, and experiences of, emancipatory practices in the past, present, and future. This imperative becomes even more essential if 'value' is the subject of theorization or if it is central to the theorization of social change. *What could be more normative than value, and what could be more paradoxical than a 'value-free' notion of value?*

The second approach thus starts with a normative definition of value independent of the way value serves the interest of the ruling order to reveal the contrast between the status quo, where the potentialities are repressed, and the desired status where value is realized by the free associations of value makers in a socio-ecological context structured and actualized as commons. This perspective has more direct implications for praxis but requires us to establish a normative notional framework for defining value by drawing on human aspirations and struggles for a viable 'good and free life' and its associated social formations.

This is not a new endeavor. As a longstanding concern throughout history, numerous philosophers, ethicists, theosophists, and global theological movements (e.g., Judaism, Christianity, Islam, and Buddhism, especially in their initial unruly forms among many less-known struggles), as well as Indigenous cultures, have centered their worldviews and practices around valuing and embodying the essence of the 'good life.' They define it according to their transcendental or more-than-material, more-than-human belief systems and ascribe 'value' to the efforts that result in the realization of the good life. This 'good life' can be understood as a social imaginary constructed based on the negation of the material conditions of life that constitute the sources of (more than) human suffering. Recent decades have seen an insurgence of interest in embracing this perspective at the cost of deserting the analytical approach previously emphasized. Within this context, one can find a diverse range of individuals and groups, including those who challenge consumerism, as well as those who advocate for a well-being economy and post-growth reform, with notable figures like Sen, Nussbaum, Berry, Soper, and Eisenstein. In addition, more radical movements, including Indigenous groups, liberation theologians, ecofeminists, post-developmentalists, and eco-anarchists, are also present in this terrain, encompassing both activists and intellectuals. Graeber (2013, p. 238), for instance, argues for reverting to the original traditions that perceive "human beings as projects of mutual creation, value as the way such projects become meaningful to the actors, and the worlds we inhabit as emerging from those projects rather than the other way around."

However, the normative approach to value, while providing a framework for criticizing the status quo, has its own weaknesses. Such perspectives have largely failed to satisfactorily comprehend the concrete mechanisms through which capitalist relations extract and exploit value from nature, community, and labor. They have overlooked the complexities of power relations and class struggles inherent in sustaining and transforming the dominant value regime.[3] Such an approach can also be fairly criticized for being too idealistic and failing to engage with the practical difficulties of realizing an alternative system that prioritizes intrinsic value over capitalist exchange-value. Although a normative theory of value can be advantageous for drawing attention to the unjust aspects of the capitalist system, it should be supplemented by a theory that enables rigorous analysis of the material and social conditions that underlie the social construction, production, and circulation of value within capitalism.

It is crucial here to emphasize that normativity should not be solely rooted in institutionalized moral or value systems. Instead, it should also be based on ongoing critical examinations of historical and current struggles, as well as the possibilities for future emancipatory efforts.[4] Such an investigation requires the involvement of liberation humanities/ethics and social sciences, which allow for the exploration and recognition of what subaltern communities of value makers perceive as value and fight for (Graeber, 2001). It also requires the intellectual engagement of nonconformist grassroots theorists who themselves engage in conversations with their societies on the value complexes they use to ascribe worth to their collective matters. The investigation of *the immanent real* and the aspiration to *the transcendental ideal* are two sides of one coin, and organic activist-intellectuals are involved in constant dialogical exchanges between them.

Theory undertaken solely for the purpose of explanation, regardless of its critical nature, has a tendency to regress into a self-defeating historical endeavor. The fundamental aim of liberation must shape the metatheoretical assumptions that underpin the theory and be seamlessly integrated into the theory itself (Hosseini & Gills, 2020a). The task will always include answering a set of transformational questions: What alternative realities potentially/ actually exist? How are the potentialities and struggles for their realization inhibited in the current social formation? And what socio-ecological mechanisms would actualize them to the level that they would transmute the conventional reality in its totality? These are not mere auxiliary questions, and therefore, our efforts to seek their answers need to be *incorporated into our account of the dynamics of the prevailing reality*.

An integrative approach that combines both an analytical value theory and a normative one is essential. Such an integrative approach to theorizing the nature and dynamics of capital and its associated social forms, seen as the most prominent cause of ongoing global shifts and uncertainties, has significant implications for understanding current socio-ecological changes and challenges as well as effective responses.

Developing a value theory that uses a normative, praxis-oriented alternative notion of value in its critical analyses of capital would be a bold move but also vital and legitimate. Such an approach, although starting with a normative/alternative notion of value as *co-defined through involvement in lively social and dialogical praxes on the ground*, must also engage in an analysis of the status quo and show how true value is replaced with or weakened by capitalist 'fetish value.' It should also explore how re-establishing the sources of 'true value' can become a base for liberation. Not only should value be seen as a normative category, but it should also be viewed as a relational construct, one that is constantly constructed and reconstructed through power relations, social struggles, and daily negotiations and compromises.

Marx's Value: Not an Affirmative Normativity

Although Marx's value theory in *Capital* provides a detailed analysis of the inner workings and historical development of capital, it is insufficient as a 'strong' transformative theory. It primarily focuses on the evolving value forms of labor and capital under the capitalist mode of re/production by embracing a non-normative notion of value. This helps Marx follow his own epistemology by establishing his analysis based on conceptual categories derived from reality (an inverted Hegelian idealism, following the example set by Feuerbach). However, this historical realism is achieved at the cost of losing sight of the theory–praxis nexus.

Although Marx inverts Hegelian idealism in *Capital*, his work nonetheless follows Hegel's logic in the real world of human labor, replacing the *Idea* with *value* (Kieve, 1983). Like the *Idea*, value is objective but immaterial for Marx. It is, however, rooted in reality by being practically extracted out of abstract labor – as grasped in the Ricardian 'labor theory of value' (LTV) adapted by Marx – and is in a dialectical *movement* from one abstract category to another through different moments of capital's self-reproduction, which in turn imposes its logic on labor and determines its forms. This can be interpreted as Marx's "value theory of labor" (Elson, 1979). However, Marx, leaves no room for the incorporation of conceptual categories, especially a type of value, derived from the counter- and beyond capital practices of revolutionary subjects, laborers, or otherwise.

Marx reinvented value theory by adopting it from his predecessors, but he retained the perception of 'value' from capital's point of view. Neither the word 'value' nor the word 'productive' has any positive moral or material meaning in Marx's version of value theory. Value is what is valued *for* capital and not *for/by* society and the life-domain. Furthermore, the positive (linguistic) connotation associated with the term 'value' in general, and its association with 'labor' as its ultimate source in classical political economy and Marxist thought in particular, has resulted in an enduring ambiguity within the Marxian tradition – an ambiguity that persists to this day, surprisingly even among many of its revisionists and critics. Foster and Burkett (2018, p. 2) refer to this ambiguity as "the systemic conflation of two distinct meanings of value": value as intrinsic worth and value as (commodity) value.

Those disputing what should be included in the perception of the sources of value tend to ignore the fact that *from a non-capitalist point of view*, 'value under capital' (or commodity value as theorized in Marx's *Capital*) is nothing but a deficit, given that it results in the annihilation of 'inclusive good life.' Therefore, it is vital to differentiate between *'true value' as defined from a commonist point of view* as a partly experienced, partly imagined, quality of life through non-submissive social relations like in *oikos*, on the one hand, versus the so-called capitalist value. Considering the differences between the two, what our theory of value should concentrate on as its primary subject is the role of capitalist value in the destruction of true value. That is, a process of a *growing deficit in aggregate true value under capital* that we conceptualize under the title of 'fetish value.'

In short, we define 'surplus capitalist value' as the difference between the aggregate economic value extracted, directly and indirectly, out of the sources of value and the value embedded in the capital which is expended in the reproduction of those sources to sustain the reproduction of capital (see Chapter 4 for a more detailed definition). The notion of surplus value, however, inclusive of all sources of value, limits our attention to the lost capacity of these sources to reproduce themselves. Nevertheless, a more important matter disregarded in such a formulation is their lost capacity to re/produce true value, which is essential to the thriving and survival of organized life in the commonist condition of living. The notion of fetish value takes this neglected reality into account.

Marx begins with an analytical concept and concludes with an implicitly normative position. Even without critically questioning the assumed 'equilibrium' and 'free market' status, he successfully critiques bourgeois political economy by demonstrating the emergence of structural contradictions, class divisions, and inherent exploitation within capitalism. His approach also has important implications for emancipatory praxis by revealing the crisis-prone contradictions in the inner organization of capitalist society, which not only can be taken advantage of but also can serve as a checklist for post-capitalist movements to imagine a future free from these contradictions (Harvey, 2014).

However, Marx accomplishes this at the expense of giving an ideal form to 'value under capital,' which isolates capital from capitalist society and its relationship with nature (an *inner* versus *outer* dualism) and excludes other sources of value for their 'unproductiveness' within capitalist production relations. While it is reasonable for Marx to object to the inclusion of unpaid domestic and reproductive work, as well as natural resources, in his definition of value since they do not directly produce exchange-value, their indirect contribution to capitalist value production (from production to circulation) only occurs once they are already reified and fetishized.

To overcome this self-imposed constraint, we need to invert Marx's value theory by starting from a normative conception of 'value' and then, on that basis, proceeding toward a transformative 'analysis.' Such a normative value theory is not about normalizing a set of universal value complexes for humanity. Instead, it is to base a theory of reality, inclusive of diverse potentialities and contextual striving for emancipation, on an abstract notion of value. The theory achieves this by liberating the notion of value from the prevailing universalist capitalist mindset and pointing to the most essential, even though potential, sources of value. The universality of normative value is an emergent one, made and remade out of the culmination of endless strivings on the ground to achieve virtues and good life(s), rather than a universality imposed by a singular mode of livelihood (Staveren, 2001). Unlike Harvey, we do not believe this would result in serious shortcomings in our understanding of the so-called 'inner structure' since a normative notion of value opens the gates for the development of a nonduality theory of capital, that is, the negation of the duality (*inner* versus *outer*) that is rooted in the unquestioning of the fetishistic nature of capitalist value.

One could inquire as to why we employ the term 'true value' instead of 'real value.' Would the latter term not more closely align with the Marxian concept of 'real wealth'? Marx's term 'real value'[5] may suggest a pragmatic approach to normativity, implying the practical value or usefulness of something in the real world. This aligns well with Marx's view that the 'value *of*' something is determined by its usefulness or practicality in achieving a particular goal. Although 'real wealth' is not simply an accumulation of use-values for Marx,[6] it still lacks the normative element since it refers to the 'existing' productive capacity of society. Therefore, coining 'real value' based on the notion of 'real wealth' contradicts our intention of not reducing the theory to a mere concern for 'use-value' and existing social capacities as a foundation for normativity.

Moreover, while the catchphrase 'real value' of labor can refer to the socially necessary labor time required to reproduce labor power, it is not sufficient to capture the full scope of value in labor. The term 'true value' is used to expand the discussion beyond the logic of capital and to consider labor in its original commoning nature as a human creative power (see Chapter 5 in this book and also Hosseini, 2022b). It implies a critical perspective on the limitations of the capitalist framework and seeks to uncover the underlying reality that is often obscured by ideology and power structures. Therefore, the use of the term 'true value' emphasizes the importance of analyzing labor beyond the narrow framework of capital–labor relations and recognizing its broader social and historical context.[7]

Marx's LTV assumes that laborers are paid based on the socially necessary labor time required to reproduce their labor power. However, in many capitalist production relations, labor is not compensated according to its 'real value.' The differentiation between the 'real value of labor' and the value of labor (as 'variable capital') paid in wage form by capital is crucial, as it contributes to the level of exploitation and surplus value generated by capitalism.

It is important to note, however, that this analysis is still limited to the context of the capital–labor relationship under the control of capital. To fully understand the value of labor, we must also consider its 'true value,' which extends beyond the narrow confines of capitalist production. *Labor is not only shortchanged in terms of its 'real value,' but also in terms of its 'true value' lost due to its alienation from its commoning nature as a creative power.* Therefore, to fully grasp the status of labor in contemporary society, we should expand our analysis beyond the confines of 'capitalist production' and consider how labor is alienated from its commoning nature as human creative power under capital's extra-production relations.

For Marx, as well as for mainstream economists, capital functions as an engine of economic growth, historical 'progress,' and advancement. This is a consequence of the particular view of the intrinsic nature of capital, i.e., that it must not only be accumulated but constantly and systemically reproduced to continue to exist. Marx's conception of capital goes beyond the economist reductionism of his time. He not only recognizes the convertibility of capital to its various social forms but also highlights the role of unequal social power. This power is exercised through the power of ownership, such as private property, decision-making processes, and institutions. Marx brings to the analytical foreground the realities of social conflicts and power structures embedded in such processes and institutions of capital accumulation. In doing so, he reveals the actual unequal social relations of power beneath the apparently apolitical mechanical and economistic representation of the economy by bourgeois political economists.

According to recent interpretations of Marx made possible through the MEGA (*Marx–Engels Gesamtausgabe*) project, value for Marx is not just a substance in things but also (or some may say, rather) a socially necessary standard arbitrated through the process of the evaluation of things; it is thus a relational quality (Elson, 1979; Heinrich, 2021; Pitts, 2021). But under the social relations created by capital, much or most of the value created by this social product (and the 'social surplus') is 'privately' appropriated and accumulated, ostensibly to produce yet further wealth in the future. On a world scale, this constitutes *processes of the expanded reproduction of capital into all spheres of life, encountering and eventually assimilating all other modes of social existence into itself.* The expansion of capital, therefore, entails the annihilation of any other form of social existence.

Marx's insight can be applied more broadly, suggesting that all historical social systems (whether capitalist or non-capitalist) can be understood in terms of how they produce, expropriate, redistribute, and struggle over the 'social surplus.' However, the notion of 'surplus' here implies that the value produced by the communities and individuals when they are (ideally) free from subordination is the same as the value that the capitalist ruling class defines in practice, only differing in the magnitudes of what is being produced and appropriated above the level needed for the reproduction of labor power. Of course, according to Marx in *Capital*, what 'associations of free and equal producers' value for themselves, is the 'use-value,' made by 'concrete labor,' while the capitalist harvests the (abstract economic) 'exchange-value' that emerges from abstract(ed) labor. However, the word 'surplus' fails to reflect the conversion of potentialities for generating true value into actualities used to construct fetish value, which is then fictitiously perceived as true value. This is not just an excess in magnitude; it is, first and foremost, *a mutation in the essence of value.* Exploitation can continue to exist in much subtler ways, even in the absence of surplus, merely by virtue of this conversion (or better to say, a 'perversion'). For instance, automation reduces the socially necessary labor time, and thereby potentially the (capitalist) surplus value, while the 'perversion' of true value to fetish value, and thus, its annihilation rate, exponentially increases.

Capital, as a form of social relations and relationship with labor, land, and natural resources, is inherently antagonistic to *oikos*, a non-capitalist care-based mode of creativity. In the historical encounter between ever-expansionist capital and *oikos*, each representing two essentially different modes of value construction, the historical tendency is that *capital annihilates oikos.* These two forms of social relations and social modes of existence cannot coexist peacefully. Why should we believe that an attempt to define *oikos* as a source with real potentialities for generating true value is more idealistic than the analyses of the capitalist mode of commodity value production in its 'ideal average'? Both approaches (the primarily normative and the primarily analytical), when left unrelated, involve a degree of idealization or abstraction from the messy realities of socio-ecological systems of livelihood, whether by assuming the existence of a perfect market in the case of capitalism or the existence of a utopian commonwealth in the case of *oikos*.

Economic growth is both intrinsic and essential to capital's socio-historical role and is conventionally assumed to be linear and unlimited (Meadows & Club of Rome, 1972; Meadows et al., 2004). Despite the fast-growing rate of the annihilation of the remaining ecological sources of value, capital as 'fetish value in motion' and 'operation' has been exponentially growing in magnitude. True value, upon which both human and non-human lives depend, holds a greater inherent reality (despite its normative status within our theory) than the realized 'fetish value' under capital. This is because, without true value, organized life itself would cease to exist, rendering any extraction of value impossible.

The Four Major Limitations

The traditional Marxist conception of capital suffers from four major limitations *when applied* to the complex socio-ecological mechanisms and processes through which capital sustains itself, deals with its crises, and interacts with the discontented social forces that it inevitably generates. These limitations are largely rooted in the works of Marx himself and are understandable considering Marx's intentional adoption of the limited scope to critique within and beyond the mainstream political economy of his time. Another reason behind the persistence of these limitations to this day, within and outside the orthodoxy, is the tendency among many of the followers of Marx, and by extension, his critics, to view any systemic reconstruction of his value theory to understand *capitalist society* as a violation of his method. Interestingly, each one of the limitations is closely related to one of the four irreducible sources of true value (as briefly introduced in the previous chapter), which, except in the case of labor, are pushed to the background whilst being seen at best as only sources of use-value or the conditions of possibility for the economic exploitation of labor.

Capital, however, is open to reconstruction by leaving the doors open for reinventing the notion of value while maintaining Marx's metaphysical approach; in some places, by briefly acknowledging sources and determinants of value other than labor, and in other places, by implying the necessity of notional extensions. These potentialities remain unfulfilled as *Capital*'s value theory focuses on the inner structure rather than the entirety of capitalist society, despite successfully showing the sociality of capital; the hypothetical dualism of the *inner* versus the *outer* remains problematic when we aim to develop a panoramic social theory of capitalist society beyond the sole perspective provided via political economy.

In brief, the principal limitations are accounted for as follows:

First, regarding the sphere of *creativity*, the Marxian concept of capital is, by and large, centered around production relations. This limitation is due to the centrality of 'productive' labor in Marxian value theory, understood as the only ultimate source of (added) capitalist value. Feminist critics (both Marxist revisionists and post-Marxists) have long argued for the incorporation of not only reproductive labor and affective work but also the body into the definition of value. Moreover, capital extracts massive amounts of surplus value in setups other than in industrial/productive and monetized ones, which have profound impacts on production and the real economy. These 'extra-productive forms of expropriation' that, in a sense, are incredibly old (antediluvian) cannot simply be considered secondary to exploitative labor-capital relations. The rising power of (global) rentier and casino capitalist classes to appropriate astronomical amounts of wealth is a pattern that has already required many theorists to broaden their definitions of capital beyond production relations and exploitation of labor power. In the aftermath of the GFC, one of the critiques that emerged from elite figures within the financial system itself was that *much of contemporary finance lacked any social utility*.

Capital can capitalize on social commons and even more abstract commons like the 'future life,' using financial and credit devices. It also capitalizes on the miseries of alienated 'Selfs' by fabricating various meanings of life and a false sense of agency and choice; a quality that makes capital far more resilient than may have been expected from within the Marxist tradition. Capital can create 'artificial commons,' such as virtual/digital spaces where the creative work of users in the form of free information and knowledge can be 'harvested' (i.e., a contemporary euphemism for 'expropriated'). Subsequent to our present discussion, it becomes apparent that the mere act of broadening the definition of value to encompass the so-called 'unproductive' sources of value is insufficient. Furthermore, it would be misguided to assume that all such sources affect value in an identical fashion. Rather, a more pressing exigency is to elaborate a theoretical framework that elucidates the interrelationship between value as formulated *under* and *beyond* the capitalist mode of production and develop a typology of causal sources that contribute to its generation.

Second, regarding the sphere of *liveability*, Marx differentiated analytically between 'use-value' and 'exchange-value' and developed the concept of 'metabolic rift' to highlight the contradictory relationship between society and nature under capitalism. However, how his theory of value can be reconstructed to adequately reflect the ecological dynamics and dimensions of capitalist processes remains highly debated (Foster & Burkett, 2016; Moore, 2017b; Saito, 2017a; Foster & Clark, 2020). In the historically specific bourgeois economy and its sciences, those spheres that cannot be converted to financial value are often perceived as lacking value, agency, and sociality. Nature, reproductive labor, public knowledge, and social–political institutions are all perverted into the material causes of use-value in the process of producing exchange-value. Marx's *Capital* analyzes such a system (Fraser, 2014). However, Marx acknowledges the foundational role that nature plays in value production, in addition to labor, the necessities of labor's social reproduction, and the consequences of constant class struggles, socially produced knowledge, and technology as factors that determine how much surplus value can be extracted.

Once again, this limitation can be traced back to the dualism of nature versus labor, and the treatment of nature by capital as a mere background condition for the possibility of value, rather than a direct source of value. Simply expanding the notion of capitalist value to include nature will not be helpful *if* our definition of value remains confined by capitalist relations. Nature is only deprived of agency and meaning when it is isolated from human society in a dualistic mode of thinking. However, when seen as an active commons of life, deeply interconnected with human creativity, care, and conviviality, it becomes an active source of *true* value, when constantly interacting with its own human component in a socio-ecological *commons form*. Therefore, a normative–analytical theory of value should focus on the conversion/perversion of this true value to fetish value form under capital.

More recently, significant efforts have been made to identify the role of 'nature' in Marx's thought and to highlight 'ecological' analysis in the classical Marxist tradition and revisionist world-system theory of capital (Foster et al., 2010; Moore, 2015; Foster & Burkett, 2016; Moore, 2017b, 2017a, 2018; Foster & Clark, 2020). However, even with such advancements, apart from the disagreements among them, an integrative theory of value and, thereby, of capital, has not been fully developed. An integrative theory of 'value under capital' and 'value beyond capital' is expected to help us develop non-reductionist explanations of the contradictory capitalist expansions despite, and through, ecological crises.

Third, with respect to the sphere of *conviviality*, although the Marxian concept of capital highlights the hierarchical social relations that underpin production relations, it often struggles to adequately incorporate a range of inequalities other than exploitative class relations unless considering them secondary to class relations in the final analysis. This has significant implications for theorizing the aspects of social life where non-capitalist power relations remain central. Traditional Marxist attempts to theorize the state, for instance, are closely related to their class theory, which is a strength in itself but inadequate insofar as it falls short of incorporating other forms of subjugation and resistance. However, they are not clearly related to their value theory, where the state is simply seen as an epiphenomenon of capitalist relations with a role to play concerning the contradictions of the movement of (fetish) value (Desai, 2020). Marx promised but never achieved his formulation of a (value) theory of the state. As arguably still the most powerful form of social domination and control, and increasingly analyzed as tightly bound up with and acting instrumentally on behalf of the interests of capital, the current forms of state power continue to exercise new colonialist/imperialist relations both at the domestic and international levels. Indeed, vast portions of humanity, as well as myriad non-human species, may be understood to be suffering under the exploitation and oppression of the capitalist–state nexus, and not just via capital directly and the capital–labor relation of exploitation. Post-Marxian theories that attempt to address this limitation either do not engage with value theory or conflate the capitalist value derived from labor with the intrinsic value embedded in the socially reproductive relations spanning from households to the state.

Power emerges in different forms and has different faces and does not solely depend on the possession (ownership) of material resources. It is not always planned, nor merely exercised unwittingly. It is not always formed against a resisting force, as it can sometimes avoid resistance through manu-facturing consent, co-opting the dissent, or manipulating satisfaction and affection. Therefore, power can be 'manipulative,' 'exploitative,' 'extrac-tivist,' 'domineering,' (MEED), or most of the time, a combination of the four (Sharī'atī, 1976; Rahnema, 2008; Byrd, 2019). To coherently theorize the complex reality of power relations, we need to reconsider the traditional assumption that human creative power is the only active source of true value. Human sociability, inclusive of relationships with non-human beings, in the ideal state of self-sustaining autonomy and just associations or what we know as *conviviality*, is another causal source of true value. Conscientious coop-eration, as one of the essential qualities of conviviality – having evolved to significantly more sophisticated levels and thus being capable of enhancing collective more-than-human well-living – despite tensions, contests, and con-trasts, produces true value. *It is through the decommonization of this socio-historical commons that the 'coloniality of capital' is realized.*

Fourth, concerning the sphere of *alterity*, the Marxian theory of capital was originally developed to explicate *how capital sustains and reproduces itself*, along with the resulting implications for both the system and society. It, therefore, focuses primarily on the task of understanding the existing order in the most objective way possible yet still putative in some important respects. A dialectical mode of thinking, however, requires us to recognize the reality of lost capacities, denied opportunities, and suppressed agencies, as well as co-opted decencies and the conflicts historically necessary for the survival of capital, without which the existing order could not be sustained. Above all are the capacities and forms of knowledge and practices that, when real-ized, could liberate us and the planet from the detrimental forces of alienated nature, history, society, and self. These fundamental sources of what we call *alterity*, therefore, remain largely under-theorized in the Marxian theory of value. No theory is constructed to show what role these sources of *alterity*, *such as human collective prefigurative actions*, do/can play in the production of forms of value that are incommensurable with value under capital.

Marx, in the process of outlining his theory of value, sporadically refers to non-capitalist modes of production and distribution (such as actually existing primitive forms of communism and imagined post-capitalist ones). However, these references are primarily used to expound the specificities of capitalist inner workings. What is more important is an integrated theory that reveals the complex yet critical relationships between the commoning sources of true value and the decommonizing mechanisms of fetish value. An alternative theory should explain how capital distorts and prevents the mechanisms of the production of true value from functioning *as transmutative projects*. It should also analyze how capital harnesses its energies by ultimately incorporating them into the production of fetish value, and what capacities exist for true value to historically overcome fetish value. Social striving to realize post-capitalist alternatives draws on humans' prefigurative power as another causal source of true value. These need to be integrated into our understanding of capital since the actuality and consequences of their denial are as real as the reality of capital and its actual ramifications for 'quality of life.' Che Guevara's maxim 'Be realistic, demand the impossible' denotes the cruel reality of denied possibilities (the impossible) in a context where the imposed/induced 'possible' is impractical and detrimental, indeed, destructive, for the oppressed common.

When We See the 'Source of Value' as the 'Cause of Value'

The limitations outlined above can be dealt with by radically reconstructing Marx's value theory of capital. However, there are important capacities nascently developed in *Capital* that can be employed on the way and further extended explicitly in dialogue with more recent theoretical developments to construct a more useful contemporary analytical framework. Even if it is an initial step, Marx's *Capital* and *Grundrisse* represent a significant move toward understanding capital's inner logic, dynamics, forms, flaws, failures, and future(s). There are potentialities in his work that have not been fully recognized, even by himself, due to the historical specificities of the nineteenth-century capitalist relations and the insufficiency and constraints of old conceptual language that influenced Marx and many who followed him. Although many Marxist and post-Marxist thinkers have made highly important progress in further addressing the complexities of capital in later decades right up until today, integrative efforts across these new developments to overcome the avoidable chasms in the tradition have remained insignificant.

The four limitations above are rooted in the underlying perception of 'value' and its 'sources.' There is a significant difference between conceptualizing value as it is actualized through the mechanisms of sustaining the prevailing power structure and defining it independent of the parameters of the reigning order in its normative form. The former may only be useful enough to display inherent contradictions of what we have hypothetically isolated as the 'ideal average' of the status quo, whereas the latter can widen the scope of the project large enough to liberate our perception of capital (including the one in *Capital*) from its self-imposed constraints, thus paving the way for incorporating other causal sources of value. However, the latter cannot be the basis for a theory that aims to be critically analytical of how the former is attained. The two must complement one another in an integrative theory.

The former notion of value has been adopted by the Marxian tradition, as well as its revisionists and critics, which we complement with the concept of 'fetish value': *the value that is not only the result of but also results in damaging the more-than-human capacities to generate true value.* This definition is crucial to make possible the synthesis between the original Marxian value theory and critical theories disappointed with its narrowness. The *commonist approach* we advocate will be based on differentiating between fetish value, capitalist value, commodity value, and true value. It does not require the negation of Marx/Marxian theory of value since it still includes its notion of value to be complemented with fetish value relative to true value and to be located in broader realms of more-than-human creativity, liveability, conviviality, and alterity.

Fetish value is inclusive of but not limited to the abstract economic (exchange) value of commodities. It is broad enough to include relations outside the capitalist mode of production itself. *Fetish value is thus understood as a quality attributed to the results of any decommoning activity under capital, which is socially fetishized to appear to have an intrinsic value for the well-being of the individuals and collectives involved.* It thus functions against their true value. *True value*, on the other hand, is *any quality definitive and advantageous for the survival, self-fulfillments, and liberation of more-than-human organized life if and only if:* (1) it is decided and realized in the most consensual, context-specific, collaborative way possible (*consensual feature*); and (2) it challenges the mechanisms of the construction of fetish value to their core (*de-fetishizing feature*). The latter condition is essential to avoid the widespread delusion that any activity beneficial to the material and psychological survival of the human community that happens in conjunction or symbiotic relationships with capital would be *intrinsically* 'transformative.' This differentiates between non-transformative and transformative true value.

The word 'source' (of value) is widely used in both classical political economy and Marxian literature. However, despite being the subject of great controversy as to what should be seen as the 'source' of value, surprisingly, extremely limited reflections have been made on what the term 'source' here really means. A source of a thing, by definition, is its 'point of origin or procurement' or the 'generative force' behind it.[8] Therefore, the source of an object maintains an 'existential causal' relationship with it, implying that the existence of the object is contingent upon its source and the causal process through which the object emerges from its source. This is different from other types of causalities, commonly referred to in mainstream social sciences, which relate already existing events/entities through probabilistic or constant conjunctions. The existential causation of an object is the most irreducible type of causality, through which the effects 'emerge' out of causes through a transformative process. This way of conceptualizing 'source' invites us to consider the application of the Aristotelian doctrine of four (irreducible types of) existential causation, i.e., the 'efficient,' the 'material,' the 'formal,' and the 'final.'

Therefore, the four causal sources of true value can be classified as follows:

(1) The commoning sources of *creativity* as the *efficient* cause of true value, comprise (more than) humans' capacities to achieve self-sustaining levels of collective well-living conscientiously and creatively in a balanced coexistence with the rest of the life-domain. These sources include humans' creative power to produce and regenerate material goods and services and to socially reproduce their own power, but also to creatively engage in leisure, play, love, and works of aesthetic, spiritual, introspective, and amusing value.

(2) The commoning sources of *liveability* as the *material* cause of true value that are the physical and intangible resources necessary for a good life. These resources are reproduced through restorative and regenerative practices that are shared and decided upon collectively by communities of organisms. The more-than-human world is a living organism beset with energy, agency, feeling, and meaning, and thus constantly generates true value.

(3) The commoning sources of *conviviality* as the *formal* cause of true value that are the capacity of (more than) human populations to develop harmonious ways of 'living well together' (well-living), self-love/care, and care for the other, as well as their relative autonomy and deep interdependence, pluriversality of their lifeworlds, and their communal solidarity. True value is the blood of communal relationships, flowing from one commons to another and back again. In the commonist state of living, any value extracted is mutually compensated with value injected so the commons and the relationships between them would persist. And finally,

(4) The commoning sources of *alterity* as the *final* cause of true value, such as organized prefigurative practices and subjectivities (imaginative, symbolic, proactivist), are essential for transcending the dominant hierarchical structures and for realizing rightful ideals and dreams and human liberation from alienating structures. Such practices are organized in ways other than, and in the categorical negation of, the capitalist, colonialist, and modernist modes of living. Any emancipatory knowledge associated with such practices, when co-created in a commons form, contributes to this final cause. A final cause is a potentiality that actualizes itself by encoding its logic into the other three fundamental causes. In a capitalist social formation, the real end of value production is the perpetuation of

capital, and thus, of capital's social power. The process of 'value production under capital' is therefore a closed circuit and a vicious cycle.

Capital, as the final cause of fetish value production, actualizes its potentiality by bringing about a transformation in the very essence of labor, nature, and community, enabling their incorporation into its machines and rendering them the means for the social reproduction of capital. Capital does not tolerate *alterity*. In our view, *alterity* is the capacity to break the closed circuit of the reproduction of fetish value. *If existential liberation is what true value is ultimately for,* and *if to be free is to be able to surpass the given world toward an open future* (Beauvoir, 2015, p. 97), then *alterity* is the *ultimate purpose* (existential liberation) in its potential/virtual form, active throughout the production of true value and the unraveling of fetish value. The bearers of this final cause of true value are prefigurative socio-political actions that counter the hegemonic *'power (structure and organization) of capital.'* By embracing alterity, individuals and communities strive to break free from oppressive systems, dismantle hierarchical structures, and foster inclusive relationships based on equality, justice, and respect. It involves recognizing the need for change, valuing diverse contributions, and actively working toward creating a more inclusive and empowering society.

The final cause differs essentially from the other three (Aristotelian) types of causality. The final cause of a thing underpins, emerges/transcends out of, and influences, the other fundamental causes of it. Final causes underpin the other three types of causes by implanting their logic in them and reshaping them so that the *end would self-realize*. Since causality is a transitional process, the efficient, the material, and the formal need to be re/coded from the onset to become the means to the end.[9]

Under the *commonist state of alterity*, true value differs essentially from fetish value by being an open-ended end (an indeterminate final cause), to be constantly defined and redefined, made, and remade. This is because the ability to prefigure, deliberate, define, and realize it in the most creative, convivial, autonomous, and ecologically liveable ways possible is itself part of the value. In contrast, under capital, value is determined by the existence of capital itself, with capital being regarded as the ultimate value. Capital thus imposes itself as a closed-ended final cause, one that imposes its fixed logic on the way social–ecological relations are organized. This requires capital to take away socio-ecological agency from the more-than-human potential producers of true value.

Marx took important steps toward freeing our understanding of capital from the bourgeois mindset embedded in the orthodox economics of his predecessors. However, as the above limitations imply, the orthodox Marxian conceptions of capital, in some important ways, remain captive to a positivistic conviction where capitalist relations are normalized in the absence of a normative perception of value. Transformative movements thus need to liberate their understanding of value from using such persisting conceptual residues as a base for defining capital and capitalism.

Surely, it is not adequate to only develop a taxonomy of the irreducible sources of value. A value theory of capital and capitalist societies needs to be based on a framework that helps us explore the 'systematic interrelations' between the four modes of causality (see Figure 2.1).

The common essence that underpins all four sources, thus making them the origin of true value, is nothing but their commoning nature. However, what makes them different yet complementary is their differences regarding the type of causality they bear. *True value, to be generated, needs each of the four types of causation to work at the same time.* The four fundamental commoning sources of true value are deeply intertwined and interdependent by virtue of their common nature and their complementary differences. The full transformation of each into capital is not possible without transforming the others, and the meaningful, sustainable liberation of one is not possible without liberating the others.

Marx's *Capital* shows some important capacities within its limited scope of focusing on the inner structure of capital and seeing how labor loses its role as an active cause (αἴτιος, aítios, meaning agent), of value under productive capital. Marx acknowledges the role of several determining factors (αἴτιον, aítion) other than labor despite factoring them out in his final analysis of commodity value (see Chapter 5 for more discussion). For instance, abstract economic (exchange) value cannot become known unless commodities are exchanged in the market, and this opens the door for other social factors and non-production relations mediated by money to play a role; factors like the subjective preferences of final consumers when defining the utility of commodities, purchasing power of workers and their families (more broadly, aggregate demand), technological advancements and automation, natural

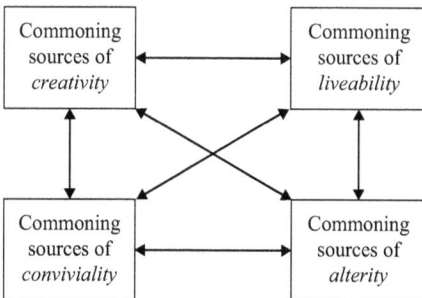

Figure 2.1 Interdependence of the four fundamental commoning causes of true value.

resource scarcity, and the metabolic rifts and damages to the environment, and socio-political struggles, and conflicts, especially between working classes and capitalist classes over wages and working hours, etc.

As a closing remark, reducing the complex social and ecological causes of value to merely economic factors is an ontological reduction with practical consequences. When translated into policy or practice, it reduces socio-ecological relations to reified material exchanges between humans and strips labor and social life of any non-material, post-human, meaning, and emancipatory potential.

Notes

1 This chapter draws on material from the paper titled *Capital as 'Fetish Value' Has No 'True Value'* by Hosseini (2022a).
2 Since the mid-twentieth century, a growing number of scholars from both the Marxist and non-Marxist camps have increasingly criticized and contested the value theory, citing its limitations and uncertainties.
3 Although Jason W. Moore's approach (2015; Patel & Moore, 2018) represents a departure from the norm, it is not without its own set of issues. In Chapter 6, we will examine these problems more closely (see also Foster & Burkett, 2018).
4 Such an inquiry would require a dialogue between the 'immanent ontology of normativity' (those values embedded in the historicity of struggles) and the 'transcendental argumentations' (as promoted through meta-ideological and meta-faith systems of thought), instead of negating one in favor of the other.
5 In both *Grundrisse*, and *Capital*, Marx uses the term 'real value' only as a catch-phrase to refer to the exchange-value of commodities different to their nominal/price/money value (1993, p. 137).
6 Marx defines "real wealth" as "the developed productive power of all individuals" (1993, p. 708). Real wealth for him is the result of social cooperation and the development of technology and productive forces and is a measure of the productive capacity of society as a whole.
7 In contrast to the term 'real value,' the term 'true value' suggests a broader perspective that goes beyond reducing the issue to usefulness or productive capacity. This aligns more closely with our perspective of dialectical critical realism, which we adopted in this book (see Chapter 3 on critical realism can help us reconstruct Marx's value theory). Critical realism asserts that there is a mind-independent reality that exists beyond human perception, but it is in a dialectical relationship with it. Marx's approach does not reject the existence of a mind-independent reality, but rather, critiques the way in which capitalism distorts and obscures this reality. Thus, Marx's approach can be seen as a form of critical realism that seeks to uncover the underlying reality often obscured by ideology and power structures.
8 See Miriam-Webster dictionary (online at: https://www.merriam-webster.com/dictionary/source).
9 "Aristotle described the causal equation as the progression from actual to potential, [from] the purity of actual desire to the modifications necessary for the realization in the potential" (Levine, 2021, p. 137).

3 Toward a Modular Conception of Capital

A Metatheoretical Discussion

This chapter and the next lay the foundations for a novel model for the theorization of capital, which we call the 'modular approach.' We pursue three goals here. Firstly, we aim to establish an analytical model that translates our normative–analytical value theory of capital into an integrative social theory of capitalist socio-ecological relations, inclusive of counter- and post-capital praxes. As argued previously, Marxist value theories, due to their focus on the 'inner structure' analytically isolated from the remainder of socio-ecological relations, are inadequate in this respect. This separation of the inner and outer resulted in the unproductive division between the theoretical and revolutionary Marx (or the so-called idealist 'young Marx' and the materialist 'older Marx)' in both public and academic discourses (Pomeroy, 2004, pp. 4–5).

Secondly, we aim to create an integrative conceptual platform that provides a space for the critical examination and dialogue of various Marxian and post-Marxist theories of capitalism, including left ecocentrism, anti-imperialism, post-colonialism, post-developmentalism, and post-anthropocentrism. This platform can facilitate a more nuanced understanding of these theories and their interrelationships, ultimately contributing to the advancement of a more synergizing transformative scholarship in the field. What makes this possible is the differentiation between our expanded notion of 'fetish value' (i.e., the capitalist value extracted out of the four fundamental commoning sources of organized life, and not just out of labor, through 'decommonizing' them) and 'true value,' as a normative concept rooted in perceiving these sources as the complementary causal sources of reproducing good life as far as they are liberated from capital's MEED relations.

Thirdly, we aim to provide a general base for co-developing context-specific, normative-yet-analytical, praxis-oriented 'theories of transformational change.' This can also be used as a methodological tool to critically map and detect the dispositions of transformative movements and forces in the pluriverse relative to one another and to capital.

Capital entails a set of radically interrelated social relational and socio-historical processes and mechanisms. The nature of capital is not only processual but also modular, meaning that capital engages manifold interactive socio-ecological processes. Multiple theories have been developed to provide explanations of these processes. However, the multisystemic mechanisms

DOI: 10.4324/9781003340386-3

through which these processes 'interface' and their constantly evolving relative positions to one another (the 'architecture of capital') have not previously been the subject of integrative theorization. On the other hand, producing an all-inclusive fixed definition has become unfeasible, and even pointless, since the modularity of network systems of capital has significantly increased. The modular nature of capitalist relations thus requires a modular approach to (re) defining capital. Such a construct enables us to better understand how the manifold theories in the literature relate to each other (Peneder, 2009, p. 93). According to Schilling (2000, p. 312):

> Modularity is a general systems concept: it is a continuum describing the degree to which a system's components can be separated and recombined, and it refers both to the tightness of coupling between components and the degree to which the "rules" of the system architecture enable (or prohibit) the mixing and matching of components.

Our approach to developing a modular explanatory framework assumes that no organically evolved social formation can be a closed system, and therefore, the aim of theory should not simply be reduced to deductive inferences around constant conjunctions of events. However, hierarchical social formations (such as slavery, feudalism, capitalism, statism, and their subtypes) are all systems of subjugation that enforce closure by creating self-serving closed circuits of fetish value production and actively suppressing and perverting any forces that threaten such closure.

A new conception of capital, suitable for theorizing capitalist social relations and societies, needs to be delineated in a modular construct consisting of elements/subdivides that are analytically distinguished to represent the reality of capital heuristically, in an ideal–typical manner. A modular definition of capital redefines the concept in the form of ideally constructed modules of interdependent social mechanisms. In this way, capital is analytically deconstructed into its constituent processes (modules) and is discussed closely in association with counter-capital processes, thus perceived as a dynamic rather than a fixed notion. Capital and its antipodal social forms are profoundly entangled, both historically and ideologically. Therefore, the new modular model has a double manifestation, contrasted from one another only for analytical purposes (see Figures 4.1 and 4.2).

In summary, based on this new model, the complete process of building and utilizing 'fetish value,' that is, *decommonization*, involves converting what is a causal source of 'true value' (in the commonist state of being) into a source of 'fetish value' (under capital). As described in detail in the next chapter, this process of perversion is composed of the reification, fetishization, and appropriation of the commoning sources of true value. These commoning sources, when transformed under capital, are turned into sources of fetish value.

Measures to Build a Modular Framework

The modular framework of analysis is intended to provide a coherent analytical structure for our commonist theory of value by capturing the nature, process, and architecture of capital vis-à-vis counter-capital. It intended to represent the processual nature of the generation of fetish value and its inherent degeneration of true value under capital by analyzing the causal mechanisms and powers that underpin the process. To achieve this, we need to take the following four measures:

First, we must broaden the notion of the 'source' or cause of value to encompass all four Aristotelian causal sources, going beyond labor and industrial production. As we discussed in the previous chapter, the new notion of 'value source' inspired by the Aristotelian doctrine of causality not only enables us to recognize other types of value sources beyond labor as forms of human creativity with efficient causal power under capital (thus acknowledging the multiplicity of sources) but also the multi-processual nature of causality through which fetish value is generated and true value is degenerated (or vice versa).[1]

Second, we should seek to define and incorporate the normative notion of 'true value' (in contrast to fetish value) as a real potentiality (under the partly imagined and partly actualized commonist state of being/becoming) perverted under capital. The previous two chapters argued for and elaborated on this measure. The commonist condition is where the four commoning sources of true value are adequately free(d) from MEED relations (whether capitalist or non-capitalist). Such a state is a paradigm of possible worlds that have real historical lineages in the past and present collective dreams and imaginations, as well as socio-ecological mechanisms deeply embedded in reality, with the causal capacity to be actualized as post-capital modes of living in and as commons.

This is not an imagined 'state of nature' as presumed in classical theories, but rather what has historically been strived for, captured in cultures of resistance and emancipation in myriad forms (from prehistoric Indigenous dreams and narratives to philosophical argumentations about the good life in the East and the West, to theological movements of the Middle East, to utopian literature and artworks, historical legacies of lost causes, and today's burgeoning pluriverse of post-capitalist movements and new efforts to retain the lost causes), but also relatively realized in different contexts and episodes (like in numerous partly failed, partly flourished experimented projects of real utopias). Since the concept of true value is normative, it requires a theory of morality to underpin its ontological source of normativity. This, as explained later in this chapter, is beyond the scope of the present book. Advancements in liberation ethics contain rich sources of insights for this purpose.[2]

The third measure is to adapt the critical realist methodology and its stratified ontology to understand how capital functions through 'causal powers' in the process of socio-ecologically reproducing itself. We will then be able to theorize the capitalist 'perversion' of both true value and its commoning sources by applying critical realist methods, especially of retroduction. Retroduction, which is central to the critical realist logic of discovery/inquiry,[3] is about postulating real, and sometimes invisible, socio-ecological mechanisms as the causal entities that can potentially trigger or give rise to events (Mukumbang, 2021).

The fourth measure involves taking a nondualist approach to capital, which views it as a phenomenon that is more sophisticated than just the real abstraction of labor and the extraction of value within its own domain. To comprehend the totality of capitalism as a social formation, we need to examine the contradictory integration between the inner dynamics of capital (as originally theorized by Marx in centering capital–labor relations) and its outer workings, i.e., the sociohistorical mechanisms that structure the relationship between capital and society–ecology. Capital constructs fetish value, which in return functions as a final cause in directing social and ecological mechanisms to sustain the process of *perversion* and turn its self-created socio-ecological crises into opportunities for its own reinvention and reproduction. Transformation in social formations cannot be sufficiently understood by theorizing the interplay between the processes of structural change ('morphogenesis') and processes of structural stability ('morphostasis').[4] To exist, the capitalist social formation inherently depends on the ability of capital to constantly grow not only in mass by extracting and accumulating surplus capitalist value but more existentially through perverting and subsuming commons into its machinery of fetish value production.

As outlined in our modular framework in the next chapter, there are (meta) mechanisms at work that underpin the unrelenting and continual social and ecological invasiveness of capital. However, at the same time, the contradictions also grow since the demolition of true value is the root cause of all socio-ecological vices. These mechanisms are not only morphological (structural/formal) but also efficient, material/substantial, and teleological. With the increase in contradictions, necrotic and counter-mechanisms become active, which stimulates the system to seek stability through negative feedback loops. Drawing on the four-fold causality model, *decommonization* can be seen as an (infra)process that is *not merely a change in the morphology of fundamental commons of true value (formal change) but also in their substance (material change), their efficacy/subjectivity (efficient change), and their purpose/ends or ultimate functions (teleological change).*

Piecing Together Traditions

How then, would implementing the above four measures lead to an ontologically coherent theory of value? Answering this question requires a deep understanding of the connections between Marx's approach to causal explanation, critical realism (CR) as both a meta-theory and a method of causal analysis, the Aristotelian doctrine of causality, and normative social theory, which encompasses the immanent, transcendent, and post-normative critique. Metatheoretical debates on the commensurability of these traditions and their ability to be integrated into an analytical framework continue to evolve, and differences are yet to be resolved (Pratten, 2009; Banfield, 2015; Vandenberghe, 2019). Rather than entering into these debates, which are beyond the scope of this book, we adopt a pragmatic approach to constructing our modular framework by piecing together those elements of the above traditions that are confidently compatible and complementary to each other. After all, these traditions have historically influenced each other. The following subsections briefly discuss the intersections between the above traditions in pairs that we can use to construct our modular framework.

Regarding the Intersection between CR in Social Sciences and the Aristotelian Doctrine of Causality

The Aristotelian terminology of four causes has often been used, most notably by Bhaskar (one of the originators of CR) and some other critical realists (Marsden, 1999; Pratten, 2009; Banfield, 2015; Bhaskar, 2018). However, the doctrine has not been systematically and coherently incorporated into critical realist discussion of methodology, resulting in inconsistencies in its use. This seems partly because of the difficulties and misunderstandings in interpreting and applying the taxonomy of causes to complex social topics and partly the result of the dominant substantial ontology that underpins its application.[5]

The use of the Aristotelian four-fold typology of causality (if applied under a more pronounced processual ontological perspective) broadens our conceptual approach to theorizing the existential causes (sources) of value. This broadening out of the notion of causation, as critical realists like Kurki (2008, p. 219) argue, allows us to recognize *the multiplicity of causes and their interactions*, inclusive of social agents, social structures, normative and discursive contexts, purposes, desires, and reasons. This conceptual broadening should be complemented by the deepening of our conception of causality through the adoption of such a critical realist stratified ontology, as Kurki claims. This would allow us to deepen our analyses beyond the conceptual and logical relations between patterns of regular and observable events, behaviors, and perceptions by incorporating the causal power of underpinning social structures, relations, and forces (2008, pp. 196–197).

Regarding the Intersection between the Critical Realist Methodology and the Marxian Method of Analysis

The advocates of critical realism have found similarities between its ontology and the ontology that underpins the Marxian method of analysis. Marx's analysis of capital was a source of many insights for Bhaskar (Marsden, 1999, p. 40). To moderate the structuralist version of Marxism, Bhaskar drew on the Aristotelian theory of transformative agency, which also underpinned 'young'

Marx's philosophical anthropology (Vandenberghe, 2019, p. 320). According to Marx, human agency has an intrinsic causal power (praxis) that is productive, creative, and communicative; an inherently transformative potentiality able to work on the pre-existing structures while being conditioned by them. However, the causal powers of capitalist structure turn human praxis into alienation, and thereby capital's reproduction substitutes for meaningful transformation.

In earlier works of critical realists, there was more application of Marxist theory to legitimize and clarify CR philosophy, whereas fewer Marxian theorists used CR as a means to advance their own theories. The more recent postpositivist developments in the philosophy of science, particularly CR, provide suitable insights for reconstructing Marxian value theory as an explanatory means to theorize socio-ecological change under and beyond the hegemony of capital.[6] Marx's value theory, as Blackledge (2015) reminds us, accounts for the dynamics of capital and explains 'tendencies' (rather than 'constant conjunctions') within capitalism. The ontological underpinnings of explanatory argumentations in *Capital* are commensurable with those of CR, despite some differences that continue to fuel productive dialogues between the two (Fleetwood, 2002; Bhaskar & Callinicos, 2003). The Marxian differentiation between the form of appearance and essence is built upon the assumption that empirical observations are not the only aim of social sciences and that *the comprehension of complex concrete processes requires an understanding of the causal powers of their underpinning structures, mechanisms, processes, and the involved social agents such as classes* (Kurki, 2020).

As Fleetwood (2002, pp. 66–67) explains, the metatheoretical assumptions of the *qualitative* version[7] of Marx's value theory are compatible with the critical realist 'stratified ontology' of '*emergence*'; i.e., the three strata of '*the empirical*,' such as the private exchange of commodities, '*the actual*' such as the coordination of laboring activities, and 'the real' (or '*the deep*'), such as the sociohistorical (meta)mechanisms behind the abstraction of labor and fetishization of commodities. According to critical realists, 'the deep' stratum is where the causal mechanisms are situated, whereas 'the actual' stratum, as a subset of the real, is where the events and non-events happen, and 'the empirical' stratum, a subset of the actual, is where human experiences and perceptions occur. These layers are distinct but interrelated and thus structured. The ultimate objects of inquiry are not the patterns of the events but the mechanisms and structures that generate them (Marsden, 1999). Marx 'retroduces' to a set of underlying structures and causal powers and relates them to the observable appearances of value (Chapter 5 will expand upon this subject).

The Hierarchy of Social Processes and Mechanisms

Like critical realism, *Capital*'s ontology is both processual and relational. Therefore, adapting critical realist terminologies, such as causal powers, mechanisms, and processes, is appropriate in reconstructing the Marxian approach to theorizing the re/production of value under and beyond capital. The idea of 'social mechanism'[8] has been promoted more centrally by the critical realist movement as an alternative to the once-dominant covering-law account of explanation in mechanistic materialism (Ylikoski, 2017, p. 404).[9] However, since there is no consensus about prototypical examples of mechanism-based explanation, much less a general definition, careless references to 'processes' (such as democratization) that posit certain types of outcomes as 'mechanisms' are common (2017, p. 405). Moreover, an exclusive attribution of mechanisms to 'the real' layer is another source of confusion, given the term is also widely used in causal explanations at the scale of the other two layers (i.e., the actual and the empirical).

To avoid these two types of confusion, we need to differentiate between mechanisms and processes by providing clearer definitions and also between the 'mechanisms' or 'processes' across the three different ontological layers. To make the latter differentiation clearer, we recommend adding the prefixes '*meta-*' and '*infra-*' to these terms. Each stratum/layer can also be considered internally stratified depending on the level of analytical abstraction. For instance, at the stratum of the real, the process of 'reification' and its associated mechanisms function at a deeper level than the process of 'commodification' and its associated mechanisms. Therefore, reification can be seen as an infra- (deeper) process relative to commodification, and since commodification emerges out of reification processes at a level closer to the actual, it can be seen as a meta-process relative to reification. Failing to differentiate between higher-level versus lower-level processes runs the risk of falling into reductionisms like mechanistic materialism or methodological individualism, thus losing the organistic recognition of the 'emerging' wholes as entities in themselves irreducible to causal relationships between their parts.

We define a 'process' as *a transition in the substantial/material, structural, agential-intentional, and/or functional aspects of a social entity, typically through a sequence of states*. Krotz (2007, p. 256) asserts that the term 'process' as usually used implies a temporal, linear sequence of different states of development in a rather well-determined dimension, with a clear starting point and direction. This would limit the applicability of the concept in the cases of *long-term complex developments* characterized *by no clear starting point, direction, or contours, which are not confined to an era or culture*. Krotz suggests the term 'meta-process' instead to refer to such developments. Examples of meta-processes are mediatization, commercialization, industrialization, and globalization. Here, we follow Krotz's suggestion to refer to causal processes of such characteristics and add that meta-processes are more *fluid, flexible constructs with the power to self-sustain and hybridize with other processes*. However, the processes that we aim to theorize through our modular framework have other characteristics that cannot be grasped by adding the prefix '*meta-*.' They are *deeper and more abstract and entail* changes in the *'essence'/nature and/or the 'form'/morphology/architecture of the fundamental sources of value*. We thus suggest the use of the term 'infra-process' to refer to the processes that underpin (meta-)processes.

By 'infra-process' we mean *a sequence of transitions in the relational reality of socio-ecological phenomena that result in substantial changes in their form and/or essence/nature*. The primary objective of our theory is to delineate the emergence of capital as fetish value. This involves examining the four commoning causes of value, which are subject to infra-processual changes under the title of 'decommonization.' On the other hand, through the commonization process, capital itself is subject to change (see Figures 4.1 and 4.2). The prefixes *infra-* and *meta-* need to be chosen relative to the level of analysis. Infra-processes underpin meta-processes, and meta-processes emerge out of infra-processes as the result of deeper substantial shifts. For instance, *reification* is an infra-process for *commodification* (there is no commodification without reification), which is an infra-process for *economic liberalization*, which itself is an infra-process for *economic globalization*. Moving backward, in order, each process emerges as a meta-process out of its underpinning infra-processes. Infra-processes therefore 'necessitate' (rather than causally originate) meta-processes by preparing the necessary (though possibly inadequate) prerequisites for their 'emergence' (see Figure 3.1). Hence, not every instance of reification leads to commodification.

A causal mechanism is typically perceived as a series of intervening means, conditions, or processes that mediate between a cause and its effects, utilizing the properties and powers of the involved entities and events (Gross, 2009, p. 364).[10] These mechanisms exist at various levels of reality and thus cannot be reduced to one another. To emphasize the stratified nature of mechanisms, some critical realists propose using the term 'meta-mechanism' to refer to more complex mechanisms that clarify "the generation of multiple proximate mechanisms that reproduce a particular relationship in different places and at different times" (Ylikoski, 2017, p. 407).

Returning to Marx, his concept of 'tendencies' is based on the *trans-factuality* of causal processes, mechanisms, and their powers[11] and their

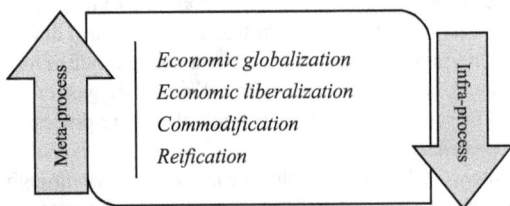

Figure 3.1 The relativity of infra- versus meta- in the hierarchy of processes.

irreducibility to the layer of actual events and empirically detectable experiences that they generate and govern. Marx's modal metaphysics is founded on "admitting unrealized possibilities and simultaneous alternate possibilities" (or what is currently referred to as the "paradigm of 'possible worlds'") (see Sinclair, 2017, p. 2). This kind of metaphysics necessitates a specific mode of explanation, namely 'contrastive explanation,' which critical realists believe is an explanation that contrasts the ways mechanisms and social structures generate new relations in different social formations (answering the question of 'why this rather than that,' rather than the simpler question of 'why this'). Therefore, explaining how social relations of production are coordinated under capitalism and how (fetish) value is generated and appropriated necessitates comparing these relations with those under non-capitalist modes of production, particularly the commoning sources of authentic value. The *qualitative* version of Marxian value theory relies on many informative contrasts.

Marx, in *Capital*, discusses the pre- or non-capitalist (natural) conditions of production and circulation of value, often sporadically, and in some places, like in *Volume 3*, more focused, to explain the unique features of the capitalist mode of production. The scope of his contrastive explanations covers a broad range of cases, each with its own revealing qualities, from the primitive communities of hunters in North America and free Americans of the colonies to the ancient and medieval communities of farmers to nomadic societies of Asia, to ancient communes and the Paris commune, and even slavery and serfdom-based production, as well as antiquated forms of interest-bearing capital. In *Grundrisse* (1973), Marx compares different capitalist conditions of production, for instance, when a road is built by a capitalist versus when it is built by a government. His *Ethnological Notebooks* (1974) studies the question of "the forms of the common" based on a historical vision that is not reducible to Western experiences (Basso, 2015, p. 3).

Concerning the Intersection between Normative Social Theory and Marxian Value Theory

The aforementioned contrastive explanations of the specific differences between capitalist and non-capitalist social formations are used by Marx to explicate the determinate characteristics of value production under capitalist conditions. However, none of these is systematically integrated into building a single theory that would explain the dynamics of the relationship between the two modes of value creation. No alternative (normative) notion of value beyond what is constructed under capital thus takes part in the value theory. No explicit normativity is designated to these non-capitalist modes of production, even in the case of the so-called imagined "associations of free and equal producers," which Marx objectively referred to in order to shed light on the specificities of capital, rather than to outline an alternative mode of value creation (Marx, 1990, pp. 171–172).

As Bhaskar (1986) argues, social theory needs to have emancipatory intent, and that emancipation depends on the critical explanation of social phenomena and their emergent properties. However, the emancipatory intent also needs to be built into the theory by explaining how the potentially and actually emancipatory properties of social relations and actions are (or can be) lost or gained in the social reproduction processes dominated by a mode of value creation.

To detect these properties, concepts need to be liberated from the meanings that the system imposes on them. 'Value' as defined in both classical political economy and its Marxian critique bears the same quality: it does not reflect any emancipatory property in itself, since it is not redefined from a normative point of view. Therefore, when defined in this manner, our social theory becomes capable of clarifying how its emancipatory properties are lost and can be restored, what forces are at play in both directions, and how such value can be used *to liberate the colonized spheres of life by transforming capitalist systems*. If an inquiry, regardless of how critical it is, does not start by exploring the emancipatory capacities embedded in existing social relations and structures, then it would ultimately submit itself to the terms dictated by the status quo, depriving itself of a strong praxiological connotation.

A normative notion of value requires a theory of morality based on a coherent ontological foundation. For true value to be considered 'true,' it needs to be ethically sound and become the building block of a 'good life.' However, Marx does not provide us with a coherent theory of morality that we can draw on for this purpose.[12] When referring to pre-capitalist social formations, Marx bases his 'contrastive' arguments on the 'organic unity' between *individual human labor* (as their human nature), *nature*, and *community* in the pre-capitalist cases. Thus, he recognizes all three elements, in their unity, as a natural source of what can be seen as a true value even though his tone is not normative *per se*.

Marx, following Aristotle, based his principles of natural law and social justice in his critique of capitalism on both human nature and community (McCarthy, 1990). However, despite its political significance, no explicit normative theory of transformative praxis can be directly deduced from his value theory and its underlying critique of political economy (Basso, 2015, p. 2). On the other hand, critical realists – while unanimously endorsing socialist values and considering a transformative mission for their theory – are polarized regarding the normative foundations of their rational critique/ judgment between an immanentist tendency and a transcendentalist one (Vandenberghe, 2019). Adherents to the former see the utopian values and potentialities for liberation partially 'actualized' in the existing institutions and historical struggles, denying them a 'real' transcendental foundation, whereas the latter make recourse to a higher ground where normative principles are eternally and universally valid and thus independent of their actualities (2019, pp. 321–323).

Marx, like Hegel and Feuerbach, rejects the transcendental foundation for morality and critique. He takes an Aristotelian approach to ethics and social justice (McCarthy, 1990), according to which morality, instead of being about rights and responsibilities, is primarily the question of how to live in the freest, most meaningful, and most self-fulfilling way possible. Thus, moral judgment or ethics becomes a rigorous inquiry (involving politics) into the material conditions, historical forces, and factors that play a role in the realization of such a good life. However, Marx also approaches morality and social justice through the criticism of the capitalist mode of value production–distribution for failing to realize its moralist goals. This immanentist and naturalist ontology of normativity has its own problems, the most significant of which is *its failure to reconcile the critique of capital with the moral constituents of emancipatory actions and post-capital communal good life.* Marx's criticism of capitalism by drawing on its own moralist standards does not tell us much about what should be morally valued or seen to be virtuous under his ideal communist condition.

The search for and debates on the most appropriate metaphysical foundations for Marxian morality has been, and will most likely remain, a demanding struggle. Certainly, overcoming the old dilemma of perceiving the normative underpinning of 'true value' as immanent versus transcendental would remain an open-ended quest but will have no impact on the pertinence of our modular framework of analysis. This is because the modular framework is a methodological means to explain the process of how sources of value change their essence; that is, a transmutation of the essence of a substance: in our case, from being a commoning source of true value (as both the actuality and potentiality of the fundamental commons) to a source of fetish value that will then find its self-sustaining and self-augmenting motion from one form to another.

Notes

1 Kockelman (2015, p. 157) states that "while Aristotle's term 'cause' has been kept and paired with its usual complement 'effect,' it is probably better to speak in terms of 'sources' and 'destinations,' as well as 'paths,' and thereby avoid any mechanistic assumptions."

2 Among other potentially insightful resources, especially for overcoming the unproductive dualism of immanence versus transcendence in orthodox Marxist and most post-Marxist traditions (Pisters & Braidotti, 2012), one may refer to the panentheistic process metaphysics of Alfred N. Whitehead and his approach to defining value. Pomeroy (2004, p. 9), who makes an effort in this direction in her book, argues that "Marx needs Whitehead to ground his claims regarding the proper ethos and telos of human life and its productive-processive interaction with, for, and as a part of the world as a relational unity."

3 Retroduction was first invented by Aristotle and later articulated by Peirce and Hanson in the twentieth century and then adopted by critical realists (see Marsden, 1999).

4   Buckley (1967, p. 58) defines 'morphogenesis' as "those processes which tend to elaborate or change a system's given form, structure or state," and 'morphostatic' processes as those "that tend to preserve or maintain a system's form, organization, or state" (see also, Archer, 2015).

5   Earlier views of causality seem to assume causality as a one-off trajectories of change and focus on substance rather than relations and becoming. The final cause or purpose, according to Aristotle, should not be confused with human intention but instead seen as a recurring evolutionary process that is present from the onset of a project. For instance, building a house is not an isolated line of causation, but rather a retroactively present process that inherits data from past occasions and potentialities for alterity. A processual ontology approach can be useful here because it gives full reality to becoming and relations, allowing causation to be seen as a process where substantial and relational properties are moments in the process.

6   The use of 'social mechanisms' and 'causal processes' as the constitutive components of our modular framework and our argument for the development of a normative value theory may imply a metatheoretical affiliation with the so-called 'analytical Marxist' current, an intellectual movement that emerged as a result of the pioneering works of anglophone analytical philosophers G A Cohen, Jon Elster, and John Roemer in the 1970s to reshape Marxism and gained some popularity (Blackledge, 2015). We agree with some common tendencies in the current as outlined briefly by Eric Olin Wright (1994), such as the importance of systemic conceptualization and stronger commitments to non-/anti-capitalist values. However, we categorically dismiss the relevance of the core principles of analytical Marxism, i.e., their rather commonly shared 'transhistorical ontology' and their 'positive methodological' commitments.

7   As Fleetwood (2002) argues, the *quantitative* version of the Marxian LTV in *Capital Volume 1*, which aims to mathematically relate exploitation to surplus value extraction, maintains the *flat ontology* behind classical models is built upon ignoring the social actors' preferences (the subjective aspect of value), the external influences such as government policies, and the often occurring disequilibrium between inputs and outputs.

8   The notion of social mechanism has attracted considerable attention from social scientists in recent years and has been loosely used as a prototypical concept in their everyday casual vocabulary. A variety of definitions have been developed and used in a wide range of methodologies and theories.

9   It may seem ironic that the concept of 'mechanism,' which was central to the mechanistic tradition of the nineteenth century, is now widely used by those who clearly reject any mechanistic social ontology. However, both the old and new approaches to using the term share the view that "any process can be described in terms of material, physical components that work together in an organized way harmoniously and consistently" (Allen, 2017, p. 60).

10 As Gross (2009, p. 364) puts it, "[t]his sequence or set may or may not be analytically reducible to the actions of individuals who enact it, may underwrite formal or substantive causal processes, and may be observed, unobserved, or in principle unobservable."

11 'Causal power' is another term commonly used in CR which is inspired by the neo-Aristotelian tradition. According to this tradition, things are bestowed real internal properties that make them capable of affecting other things. 'Transfactuality' refers to the endurance of the efficacy of causal mechanisms across different contexts, regardless of their actualization or empirical perception. The precise effects of mechanisms in open systems, however, depend on the context, as the same mechanisms may not generate the same events in a different context. Therefore, causality is contingent in open systems. Moreover, in open systems, instead of fixed regulari-

ties, we have demi-regularities that are expected habits and tendencies that alter under countervailing conditions.

12 Marx often criticizes morality. But, as Eagleton (2011, pp. 158–159) argues, he should be seen as a critic of (bourgeois) 'moralism', an intellectual inquiry that sees (bourgeois) 'moral values' as transhistorical (divorced from sociohistorical forces and material factors) and thus a universal base for absolute moral judgement.

4 The Modular Architecture of Capital

In this chapter, we develop our modular framework by building upon the intersections between the Marxian theory of capital, critical realism, and the Aristotelian fourfold causation theory previously explored. With reference to Harvey's formulation of 'capital as value in motion and boundless accumulation,' we posit that capital is actually 'fetish value' in destructive operation built upon the boundless eradication of 'true value' and functioning as 'negative value' by eradicating the capacities of organized life for self-sustaining and thriving. Capital is thus an expansionist value regime inherently prone to conflict and struggles, but its relationship with its counter-movements that emerge out of its self-generated crises is not simply antagonistic.

Capital: A Modular, Infra-processual Conception

Decommonization begins with what we redefine as the 'perversion' of the indispensable commoning sources of true value into their reified forms (i.e., reification) and finally into capital (see Figure 4.1). The reification infra-process is complemented by the fetishization and appropriation infra-process and moderated (and thus relatively stabilized) by the civilizing meta-mechanisms. The reification infra-process makes appropriation and accumulation of extracted fetish value in its tangible forms possible. Different types or instances of capital are constructed through the combination of various modes of appropriation of its reified social forms under the fetishization infra-process (see Figure 4.1 and Table 4.1).

The models developed here operate at the level of infra-processes for the purpose of analytical simplification. For example, the process of commodification, while a meta-process in relation to reification, is not included in the model. This is because commodification is not the only process necessitated by reification, and capital does not solely rely on commodification. The role of commodification can be analyzed through the application of the model in contextualized cases.

The concept of commodification is closely tied to exchange-value and may neglect the use-value of commodified items as well as the social and ecological value of uncommodified entities. For instance, analyses that center

DOI: 10.4324/9781003340386-4

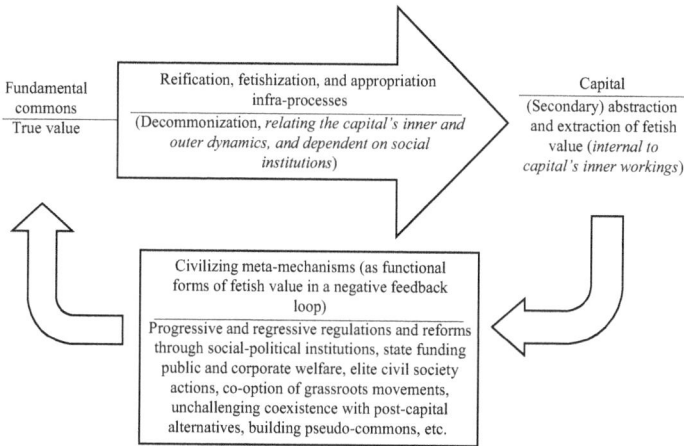

Figure 4.1 Capital as the product and infra-process of decommonizing the fundamental commoning sources of value and perverting them into sources of fetish value (to fuel the inner workings of capital).

around commodification often overlook the value of social and community services that are not traditionally exchanged in the market but are essential for both the well-being of society and the accumulation of capital. Moreover, commodification-centered analyses fail to capture how capital uses non-market mechanisms, such as state subsidies, intellectual property rights, or monopolies, to extract value, giving capitalists a considerable advantage in the market.

By starting from a deeper level, i.e., the infra-process, our theory can account for how capital transforms social and ecological relations into abstract forms of value. Thus, the scope of analysis is extended beyond the inner organization of capital, where the commodification of labor and commodification through labor, and the embedding of labor into the commodity, take place.

The reification infra-process under capitalism, which is central to decommonization, objectifies the fundamental commons by depriving them of their inherent transformative capacities and actual subjectivities as active sources of true value. This allows for their appropriation and the extraction of fetish value. Reification, as the term implies (thing-ification), is about the conversion of subjects to objects by taking away their agency and meaning. This includes a broad range of processes, such as the objectification of (more than) human powers for creativity and liveability, to what is artificially constructed as labor and nature under capital. It is this mechanism at the level of 'the deep real' that submits these commoning sources of value to socio-economic processes at the level of 'the actual,' such as commodification, commercialization, and financialization within the sphere of capital. Note that this is a broader concept than the narrower notion of reification attributed to production relations in the Marxist tradition, which is closely tied to (and even equivocally equated with) fetishism and alienation. Reification here happens outside the inner structure of productive capital as part of the decommonizing infra-process.

Fetish value is a new entity with an 'essence' different from the 'essence' of true value. The motion of fetish value within the inner organization of capital is of a non-essential nature (Tombazos, 2020), meaning the inner motion is only a trans-'formation' of the forms of appearance from one diversity to another. The reification of fundamental commons of life is an infra-process through which a (Sadrian) 'substantive motion' takes place (a transmutation in the essence of an entity, here the fundamental commons). The commoning nature of the sources of true value becomes converted into an 'essentially' different nature that functions like an object alienated from its original agency and meaning, which can only be fully realized in the commonist state of being. This is an ontological shift or perversion that requires its own new epistemology to underpin the modern sciences and technologies that treat nature as the 'object' of thought and action. Under such a 'science as ideology' (Celikates & Jaeggi, 2017), fundamental sources of liveability are ideologically re-constructed as the riches/gifts of nature through reification, to be exploited through the capitalist processes of extracting value that are built upon such an alienating instrumentalist epistemological setting.

The objectification of the subject is incomplete without placing it under the 'control' of an object that is rendered a fetish subjectivity, hence fetishization and appropriation. Such a conversion of 'subject' to object is always complemented with the conversion of 'object' to subject, thus the 'inversion' of subject and object, which we alternatively call 'abstraction.' The fetishizing infra-process works to enhance the sustainability of socio-ecological relations, through which capital is assigned irrational but legitimate incorporeal values. In this way, the expansion of capital gains roots in the human psyche as the inevitable or unrivaled source of value. Capital as fetish value now gains the status of a telos, a final cause in its own inner structure of reproduction. External to capital's inner dynamics, capitalist value complexes are normalized, moralized, and even become sources of fetishistic identity formation. They become entangled with modern versions of patriarchal, ethnocentric, anthropocentric, and colonialist value complexes, reinventing them and being reinvented by them. This is how political-cultural hegemony is created, leading to more concentration of power and the de-democratization of social institutions in the broader capitalist formation. Some key meta-mechanisms that work under this infra-process are modern anthropomorphizing, psychologizing, and sanctifying.

Consider the example of (more than) human creativity as the efficient cause of true value and its perversion into labor as a commodity under capital (Hosseini, 2022b). The meta-mechanisms of fetishization, including anthropomorphizing, psychologizing, and sanctifying, can play a significant role in this perversion/decommonization infra-process. For instance, psychologizing human creativity by framing it as an innate, individualistic talent or gift, instead of a collective social practice developed and nurtured within a community enables the commodification of creativity by reducing it to a personal attribute that can be bought and sold on the labor market. Sanctifying mechanisms can create hierarchies of talent that reflect market values, making certain forms of creative expression seem more valuable or prestigious than others. Anthropomorphizing mechanisms can encourage the development of artificial intelligence and other technologies that seek to replicate and replace human labor, contributing to the decommonization of human creativity.

Fetishization, which makes reification more than objectification, is an infra-process through which value generated under capital, i.e., fetish value, takes on the status of a 'subject' being not only sold to both value makers and takers as 'true value' through false consciousness but more importantly making them existentially dependent on it as a regulator of their social and ecological relations. This dependence is so insidious that it can blind many struggles over the redistribution of fetish value (in the form of income and wealth generated through capitalist relations) to the lost or perverted potentialities for the generation of true value. These struggles, as a result, lose their capacity to implant and pursue final causes alternative to capital.

By the term *appropriation*, we mean something deeper than dispossession or expropriation. It chiefly regards transforming common care or stewardship, where everyone is responsible for one another, into hierarchical control that delimits the purpose of the value-generation process. This process can take various forms, such as primitive enclosures or modern land grabbing, or more abstract, sophisticated methods of controlling the flow of information that is essential for value production. For example, in a capitalist factory, the appropriation of the fruits of labor is only possible if labor power is exchanged as a commodity ('secondary abstraction' as we call it here, as theorized by Marx), and if labor is already created from the decommonization of human creative power (which we call 'primary abstraction').[1]

However, appropriation does not need to happen after reification is done. These infra-processes are intertwined. Disassociating human creative power from its commonist embeddedness in the life-domain (contributing to the 'Great Rift') is a prerequisite for its alienation from the rest of the domain, and thus its objectification into labor power as a commodity. Political forces and struggles play a decisive role in this process. While an old ruling class may decline, and a new one may emerge, what happens underneath the rise and fall of ruling classes and their internal compositions is the reinvention of power structures. Hierarchies (such as patriarchal, racial, and anthropocentric) continue to reinvent themselves in a dialectical relationship with the evolutionary reinventions of the modes of extracting and appropriating value. New mechanisms are invented to make the appropriation of value more efficient. Appropriation determines power and is determined by power.

In the capitalist economic realm, appropriation mechanisms include legal and policy procedures that regulate access, ownership, and redistribution. These include property rights, corporatization, taxation, and privatization, as well as those that legalize, legitimize, and regulate risk-taking, rent-seeking, profiting, seizing, enclosure, and all mechanisms developed to sustain control over the flows of capital and its accumulation in favor of capitalist classes. These mechanisms are subject to intra-class and inter-class conflicts and are gendered and racialized, thus requiring civilizing mechanisms to maintain systemic order, as mostly implemented by the state and the elite segments of civil society. Financial 'interest' in capitalist societies is a mechanism for appropriating the future-oriented risk-taking behaviors rooted in human prefigurative power, already reified into exchangeable commitments (Christophers, 2016). Social media platforms are new tools for appropriating the affective activities of millions of socially alienated internet users, reified in data form, who seek companionship to compensate for the convivial relationships lost to the imperatives of living in estrangement.

Civilizing meta-mechanisms make up the system-wide civilizing metaprocess, which functions as a negative feedback loop to save the system from excessive disequilibrium and the escalation of chaos caused by excessive reification. Progressive redistributive mechanisms, such as taxation, subsidization, social welfare provision, environmental conservation, basic incomes, full employment, corporate long-termism, co-option of dissent (often in the form of participation), production of common goods, and building pseudo-commons (that give a false sense of communality to their participants and often are de-commonized to extract value out of their free interactions) are part of such mechanisms. Civilizing mechanisms can also include regressive measures such as the regulation of immigration, fortification of surveillance, and adoption of ethnocentric majoritarian policies. These mechanisms, whether regressive or progressive, have the power to reshape social institutions in the realm of societal relations through processes such as rationalization, regulation, standardization, institutionalization, subjectification, interpellation, and engineering consent.

A modular definition of capital extends the scope of analysis beyond exploitative production relations. The so-called productive capital, when seen from this perspective, includes not only the reification of (more than) human creative power but also the fetishizing infra-processes, which counterfeit 'true value' by manufacturing meaning, motivation, and consent in a world fast emptied of (non-capitalist) visions and true Self-value. Fetishization complements reification in decommonizing human creative, convivial-caring, and prefigurative capacities for living in balance with their commoning sources of liveability and thereby helps normalize the networks of capital's power. However, as capital cannot reach absolute supremacy due to the contradictions built into its inner workings, this results in greater dysfunctionality in the works of socio-ecological commons. Since the crises cannot be effectively managed despite orchestrating mass deceptions and delusions, capital creates more chaos, public angst, and popular dissatisfaction. Civilizing mechanisms as negative feedback loops (activated by social-democratic, radical populist, and a range of movements in between) come into play, and their diluted versions become co-opted when conflicts over the socialization of the costs of the reproduction of labor (as the reified form of human creative power alienated from its commoning origin) pose challenges to the system.

The policies and practices associated with the civilizing process are constantly influenced by internal conflicts within the capitalist class, particularly among different factions that mobilize their social bases through elections or exert their power through plutocratic influences. Additionally, inter-class conflicts arise between the subaltern class and the capitalist class, further shaping the dynamics of the civilizing process. The contention of the latter type is typically mediated, for example, via liberal democratic and collective bargaining apparatuses. When this type of contention fails to deliver due to being weakened, since capital's supremacy consumes the lower and working classes in their struggles for redistributive social justice, the regressive civilizing forces gain greater momentum. Those factions of the capitalist class that benefit from regressive civilizing mechanisms as well as the factions of working and lower classes with a strong sense of resentment and fear, make a clientelist alliance against the other factions of the capitalist and working classes (Hosseini et al., 2022).

The *decommonizing* and *civilizing* meta-processes are both complementary and contradictory to one another, creating a bipartite epicenter comprised of the major forces of 'center-right' and 'center-left' in the politics of capital. Fragile political stability is normally (albeit temporarily) achieved when the contradictory and complementary relations between the two meta-processes reach equilibrium. The center is, however, not static, as the political forces of the two sides can regain their momentum alternatively through economic cycles of growth vs. spending, recession vs. inflation, and globalization vs. deglobalization.

There is no pure or perfect state of capitalism. This partiality/imperfection is the product of its inner contradictions and the contradictions it has in its relationship with domains of life that stay out of its full domination. This is both advantageous and disadvantageous from an anti-capitalist point of view. It allows for change but also creates crises and renders capital with unparalleled self-serving dynamism and flexibility. Besides the civilizing ones, there are always resisting and transformational forces and mechanisms in place. Ideally, the counter- and post-capital mechanisms work in the opposite direction to decommonization, i.e., in the direction of converting fetish value back to true value and/or generating and circulating true value out of fundamental commoning sources. However, many such forces do not negate capital in its entirety. In the real world, the relationship between capital and counter-capital is not dualistic. Many transformative forces become willingly or unwillingly absorbed into the civilizing processes or continue to coexist symbiotically alongside capital in isolated niches until they lose their potency to survive due to capital's infiltrations or their internal exhaustion.

The circulation of true value can be interrupted at any moment by capital and diverted into fetish value production. Figure 4.2 portrays the generation of true value through the counter- and post-capitalist meta-processes of value generation, thus demarcating it only analytically from the fetish value construction in Figure 4.1. There are two ideal-type processes in place, which not only resist the decommonization trends but also function to transform the capitalist social formation by (1) restoring true value through converting capital back into fundamental commons (de-capitalization or more broadly re-commonizing), such as via community wealth mobilizations and workplace democracy, and/or preserving and protecting the existing commons against the threats of capital through resistance, disruption, and protest; and (2) originating true value out of the fundamental commons through the generation of what we call 'common graces,' which are the objective manifestations of true value in the form of enhanced qualities of living together and improved capabilities to thrive, inclusive of non-human beings (see Figure 4.2 and Table 4.1).

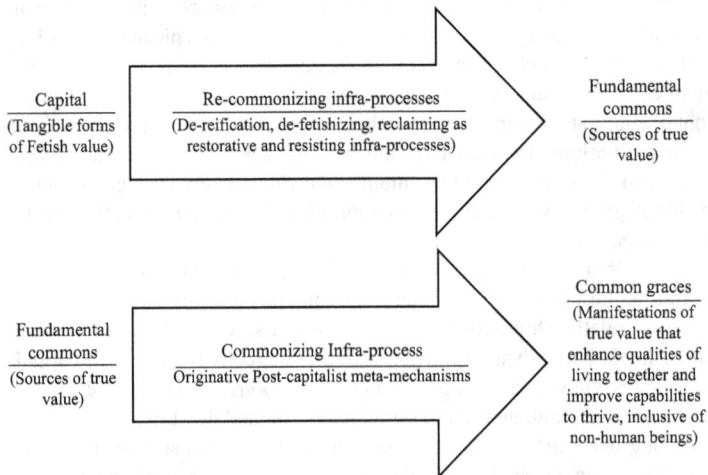

Capital (Tangible forms of Fetish value)	Re-commonizing infra-processes (De-reification, de-fetishizing, reclaiming as restorative and resisting infra-processes)	Fundamental commons (Sources of true value)

Fundamental commons (Sources of true value)	Commonizing Infra-process Originative Post-capitalist meta-mechanisms	Common graces (Manifestations of true value that enhance qualities of living together and improve capabilities to thrive, inclusive of non-human beings)

Figure 4.2 True value-generation processes, restorative and originative.

The *true value generating infra-processes* can be ideal-typically divided into two major types:

(1) The re-commonization infra-process, which comprises three restorative types of meta-mechanisms: (1) *de-fetishizing meta-mechanisms* that delegitimize the irrational incorporeal values of capitalist relations and reinforce communal bonds and solidarity, and construct liberation ethics and utopian visions. The de-fetishization process is highly pluralistic and heterodox, and it reinforces transformative resistance through the promotion of more participation, autonomy, and diversity. However, it also paradoxically ramifies and disorients transformative forces. (2) *De-reifying meta-mechanisms,* which are persistent actions that aim to resist or reverse capital's reification infra-process by restoring the lost subjectivity of the objectified sources of true value. Examples include de-commodifying, de-institutionalizing, and de-rationalizing praxes. (3) *Reclaiming meta-mechanisms* and their associated praxes are those that de-appropriate and liberate sources of value. Examples include de-privatization, nationalizing natural resources, occupying to reclaim public spaces, de-commercialization, reclaiming common goods, reclaiming the management and ownership of workplaces, the socialization of ownership, the democratization of economic spheres, restoring of commons, and the decolonization of social relationships and knowledge.

(2) The originative post-capitalist meta-mechanisms of the commonization infra-process shift the way true value is generated by giving primacy to the preservation and regenerativity of fundamental commons and their integrity in the generation of common graces within the socio-ecological boundaries of the commons. The restorative and originative praxes are interdependent; one cannot fully achieve its goals without the other one (Gills & Hosseini, 2022).

A commonist perspective requires us to explicitly distinguish the key infra-processes that constitute capital through interacting, interfacing, and contradicting one another. This cannot be complete without the consideration of social praxes and processes that are in constant tension with capital. The result will be a modular kit of distinct concepts that represent these independent but interrelated identifiable building blocks (as portrayed in Figures 4.1 and 4.2 and as summed up in Table 4.1).

As per the above modular approach, *capital* can be briefly defined as follows:

> Capital is both the product and the infra-process of perverting the fundamental causes of true value into the causes of fetish value. As the product, it is the corporeal manifestation of fetish value, and as the infra-process, it is essentially the abstraction and appropriation of fundamental commons.

Table 4.1 Capital: a modular, infra-processual conception

1. **Decommonization (cf. Figure 4.1)**
    1. **Reification infra-process:** (central to decommonization) objectifies commons capacities so they can be appropriated and transformed into capital. This necessitates the emergence of meta-mechanisms that may commodify, commercialize, and/or financialize social relations.
    2. **Fetishization infra-process** (central to decommonization) is essential for the construction of fetish value and not only its legitimization as value but also for placing it as a final cause of value production. Some key meta-mechanisms that work in association with this infra-process are modern anthropomorphizing, psychologizing, and sanctifying mechanisms.
    3. **Appropriation infra-process** (central to decommonization) includes legal and policy procedures that regulate ownership, such as property rights, corporatization, and privatization but also those that regulate risk-taking, rent-seeking, betting, profiting, seizing, enclosure, and control over the flows of capital and its accumulation in favor of the capitalist class.
2. **Civilizing meta-mechanisms** (as negative feedback loops to decommonization) address uncertainty in the system and work toward equilibrium and stability through several meta-mechanisms at the cost of softening and thus deaccelerating decommonization. These meta-mechanisms include rationalization, economic regulations, standardization, and institutionalization, such as unionization.
3. **The central meta-mechanisms of the commonist infra-process of true value generation (cf. Figure 4.2)**
    1. **Reclaiming meta-mechanisms** (central to the restorative meta-processes of re-commonization and complementary to de-fetishization and de-reification) de-appropriate and liberate sources of value. Examples are de-privatization, de-commercialization, reclaiming common goods, the socialization of ownership, the democratization of economic spheres, restoring commons, and decolonization.
    2. **De-fetishizing meta-mechanisms** (central to the restorative meta-processes of re-commonization and complementary to de-reification and reclaiming) delegitimize fetish value and unveil its negative function. Examples are movements that strive to challenge and change the value system by questioning the primacy of wealth or economic growth as a social value.
    3. **(De-)reifying meta-mechanisms** (central to the restorative meta-processes of re-commonization and complementary to de-fetishization and reclaiming commons) include praxes like de-objectification and *de-commodification*.
    4. **Originative post-capitalist meta-mechanisms** (central to the commonization infra-process) place the alterity of good life as the final cause and, thereby, shift the way true value is re/generated by giving primacy to the preservation and regeneration of fundamental commons and their integrity.

Capital functions to re/construct, sustain, and extend manipulative, exploitative, extractivist, and domineering (MEED) power structures that, in turn, uphold its supremacy as a value regime (Figure 4.3). It is socially and historically constructed through the *decommonization* process, which involves the reification, fetishization, and appropriation of commons. The civilizing meta-mechanisms act as a stabilizing factor in a negative feedback loop (Figure 4.1). Capitalist society is characterized by constant interaction between capital and various transformative forces that operate through restorative *re-commonizing* meta-mechanisms of de-reification, de-fetishization, and reclaiming meta-mechanisms, as well as *originative post-capitalist meta-mechanisms* that generate true value out of and back into fundamental commons (Figure 4.2).

From the Organic Configuration of Commoning Sources of True Value to the Mechanical Architecture of Capital

The relationships among the fundamental commoning sources of true value in the commonist state of living are characterized by their organic nature. These relationships transcend boundaries, functions, and hierarchies, facilitating decentralized flows of care, influence, and information. These commoning sources constitute a higher commons, the life-domain in commonist living, functioning like organs within an organism, drawing their vitality from collective wholeness. Under capitalism, the organic interconnections among these fundamental value sources give way to mechanistic relationships. They become compartmentalized into socio-economic, socio-ecological, socio-cultural, and socio-political categories governed by mechanical interactions. Flows of fetish value (standardized with normative power) in their major forms (economic, political, social, and ecological) are controlled by the capitalist state, big business, and finance.

Figure 4.3 combines Figures 3.1, 4.1, and 4.2 to illustrate the perversion of the organically interrelated four fundamental causes of true value into the compartmentalized architecture of capital, consisting of the four spheres of capitalist society with mechanistic relations among them.

To acknowledge that capitalist production relies not just on the exploitation of labor, but also on the expropriation of 'nature,' 'social reproduction,' and 'political prerequisites' may sound like a revelation for those who have been immersed in reductionist neoclassical economics and orthodox productivist Marxism. However, this argument still relies on these ideologically constructed bourgeois categories that normalize the alienated forms

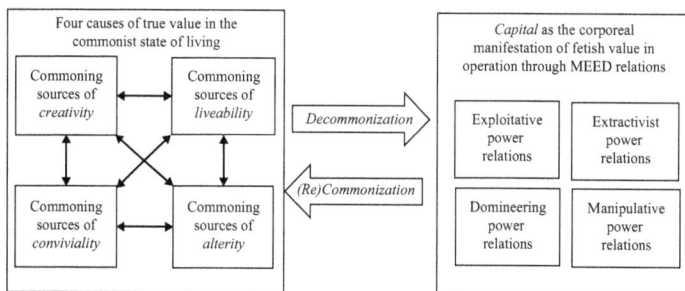

Figure 4.3 The mechanical architecture of capital versus the organic configuration of the commonist state of living.

of originally commoning sources of true value. The concept of 'nature' is an ideological construct that portrays reified and fetishized sources of live-ability, disconnected from human labor. In reality, the life-domain or what is commonly referred to as 'nature,' actively engages in creative work by con-tinuously 'actualizing' the potential for self-realization. Moreover, human labor power emanated from the human body is nurtured by the rest of life-domain and becomes an active part of it. Reluctantly employing these reductionist terms, it is the 'surplus labor' of the so-called 'nature' – quan-titatively, the energy–matter extracted per unit of natural resources within a given timeframe beyond the ecological requirements for the sustenance, regeneration, and flourishing of ecosystems – that serves as a material cause in the generation of fetish value.

Fetish value within the capitalist framework cannot arise solely from any individual fundamental commoning source without the perversion of the other three indispensable commons to create the necessary conditions for its generation. As discussed in Chapter 2, the indispensable commoning sources, despite their differences regarding their Aristotelian causal relations with value, are deeply intertwined. Therefore, *the decommonization of each fundamental commons is associated with the peripheralization or annexa-tion of other commons to the required degree.* Annexation occurs within the constantly shifting frontiers of capital, where the decommonization and appropriation of true value sources take place. It signifies the encroachment of capital into *non-commodified* zones of commoning, whereby self-regener-ating activities outside of capitalist relations are assimilated and integrated into the capitalist framework. This annexation is a crucial aspect of the colo-nialist nature of capital, as it entails the absorption and control of diverse commoning ways of living to varying degrees, contributing to the ongoing decommonization process.

Creativity in Capitality

The innate creativity of humanity constitutes a vital commons that generates true value in a commonist state of living. However, in the context of capital-ist relations, this creative force is transformed into 'labor' through the infra-process of decommonization. Consequently, labor is stripped of its subjective nature, becoming a material cause, or substance, of capitalist value. This loss of subjectivity is due to the alienation of labor from its original common-ing nature as human creativity, which should be in organic harmony with the sources of extra-human creativity, liveability, conviviality, and alterity that exist within a commoning status (refer to Chapter 5 for a detailed discussion of this argument).

Only when the focus of our analysis is on the decommonization of one of the fundamental causes of true value (e.g., creative power) should we examine the other three fundamental sources of true value in terms of the capitalist meta-mechanisms that turn them into the 'conditions of possibility' or the peripheral necessity for the primary source of value in question. In the process of extracting value out of the work of the so-called nature via algorithms and machines with the involvement of an apparently negligible amount of human labor, the latter (peripheralization of labor) becomes a condition of possibility for the former (exploitation of nature).

Take, for example, Bitcoin mining and pooling, where minimal living labor (for servicing, maintaining, and upgrading the machinery) is involved directly in the production of this financial digital asset. The production of Bitcoin relies heavily on energy consumption in processing vast amounts of data, resulting in significant environmental impacts. The primary commons that are being directly decommonized are the natural and energy resources being consumed in the process of mining. The dead labor involved in producing the necessary machines, material infrastructure, and energy resources is also expropriated, meaning that its value is appropriated without providing compensation or recognition for the laborer. The status of this expropriated labor is similar to the status of unrecognized/unwaged expropriated domestic labor in classical industrial systems. The labor directly involved in solving the hash function and providing the proof-of-work is not directly exploited either; rather, it plays a regulatory role.

> Within the strict and automatized confines of the Bitcoin algorithm, abstract labour becomes the mechanism of control [through the verification of transactions] and, consequently, its source of value ... The central authority is replaced by abstract labour as the technology of immanent control.
>
> (Tremčinský, 2022, p. 32)

The value produced through Bitcoin mining ultimately derives from the labor involved in its production, but the laborer involved is not directly exploited in the same way as classical industrial laborers. This peripheralization of labor can be seen as a form of reification of labor without its commodification, in which labor loses its subjectivity as an efficient cause by being reduced to a secondary material cause. Fetishization occurs when an object is given subjective qualities or characteristics, such as value, power, or agency, that are actually derived from social relations and practices. In the case of Bitcoin, the rhetoric around its decentralization and potential to liberate us from government surveillance is a way of fetishizing the technology. By attributing to Bitcoin qualities such as decentralization, freedom, and security, the discourse surrounding the technology presents it as a powerful and transformative force. This fetishization of Bitcoin serves to obscure the social and political dimensions of the technology and to present it as a neutral and apolitical tool that can be used to achieve a range of goals. This can make it more difficult to critically assess the impacts of the technology and to identify the interests and power relations that are at play.

Liveability in Capitality

Capital fragments the life-domain by decommonizing its sources of liveability, resulting in the alienation of human creativity from its commoning nature. Capital responds to the malaise it creates by enlarging the chasms between social spheres, which further reproduces capital, without solving socio-ecological crises. Capital fetishizes reified and dispossessed commons, selling them as solutions to alienation. These include the well-being and self-help industry, alternative medicine, anti-aging science, and ecotourism, which only exacerbate capitalist remedies for alienation (Davies, 2015; Hosseini, 2018b; Hosseini, 2021). Nature is the result of the fetishization of liveability sources, becoming an object ready for appropriation. The perversion of liveability into fetishized nature leaves less capacity for decommonization and capital's 'cures' are augmentative but narcotic based upon enchantment. This leads to increased costs and the unaffordability of alternatives.

Conviviality in Capitality

Meaningful lives, in a commonist state of living, are created when human beings autonomously explore, experience, and reflect on the *totality* and *ultimacies* of their relationships with/within their own Selfs with one another, with history, society, life, and Existence. The lack of conviviality in reified social domains, under capital, reduces individuals and communities to bearers of capitalist value, resulting in emptiness, repetitiveness, and uncertainty. Capital is not only anti-social but also paradoxically alters societal modes of livelihood, creating demand for a more meaningful life among alienated individuals. As part of its self-civilizing mechanisms, capitalism capitalizes on identity crises and alienation not only by fetishizing consumerism as a way of promoting sociability but also by offering a fetishized sphere of coexistence, such as digital communication platforms and cryptocurrencies, that extract more capitalist and fetish value. Fetishization accelerates capital's growth but also exacerbates its intrinsic crisis tendencies, leading to greater social disparities, ecological crises, and financial turbulences. To ensure its continuity, capital relies on the decommonization of social reproduction, making it imperative to unite class struggles with liberatory efforts within the realm of social reproduction for true liberation.

Alterity in Capitality

In a commonist state of becoming, the future is one of the foundational commons of all possibilities that everyone contributes to, not owned or controlled by anyone. It is a source of alterity, the final cause of true value. But when capital interferes, the future becomes objectified and fetishized as the bearer of ultimate value production, rather than a collective effort toward new possibilities. As essential commons diminish, the process of constructing new commons becomes lengthier and more demanding, contributing to a deficit in true value. For example, the value of endeavors and the consequences of inaction in addressing the global ecological crisis should be subtracted from the capitalist value produced, considering the detrimental effects it has on the environment.[2]

Capital decommonizes the future by narrowing the scope for alterity, even colonizing the future by turning future work into a commodity. Financial and monetary measures determined undemocratically play a significant role in this process. Capital strikes and hoardings prevent democratic determination and limit opportunities for social progress, undermining democratic decision-making. The labor of the future encompasses essential socio-political actions aimed at mitigating the negative impacts of capitalist value production on self-sustaining organized life. The erosion of fundamental commons leads to a deficit between capitalist value and true value, necessitating a higher amount of true value to recommonize capitalist relations and protect existing commons.

Metaphorical Arithmetic of Capital

The application of our framework to reconstructing the Marxian value theory requires two major steps: (1) differentiating between fetish value and capitalist value by incorporating the true value lost to the process of decommonization and (2) expanding the definition of capitalist value beyond the abstract labor of commodity producers to include the work emanating from the other three reified forms of fundamental commons: the expropriated work of so-called nature, community (especially social reproductive labor relations), and the work of capital's 'political organization.'[3]

Although arithmetic representations of the theory may risk oversimplification, they can be valuable tools for illustrating the proportions and relationships between the heterogeneous components of value creation under capital in a simplified manner.

In the commonist state of living, characterized by the regenerative mechanism of organized life and its ability to counteract entropy, true value experiences a surplus that extends over a significant span of geological time. This surplus value is a result of the sustainable and harmonious interactions within the ecosystem, where the re-generation and preservation of true value are prioritized.

Surplus true value under the commonist state of living = *true value produced – true value consumed by the sources of value – true value lost to entropy ± external factors or influences > 0*

The surplus true value generated can have various implications for the extension/flourishing of life, long-term sustainability, and addressing disparities among and inside the ecosystems. Surplus true value is utilized to counteract entropy and maintain vitality, prioritizing a self-sustaining status, rather than infinite growth.

Under capitalism, true value is in an exponentially growing 'deficit' due to an increase in the rate of decommonization of the four fundamental causes of true value:

Deficit true value under capital = *true value produced inside and outside capitalist production relations – true value consumed and expropriated by capital – true value lost to entropy – potential commonist true value lost to capitalist decommonization* < 0

True value can manifest within capitalist socio-ecological relations while operating outside the confines of productive capital. This can be observed in non-capitalist social and ecological reproductive activities, as well as in politically and future-oriented activism aimed at fostering communal well-being. Moreover, true value can also arise within capitalist production relations, such as when workers in a privately owned firm provide mutual care and support during challenging times or in their collective struggles for improved working conditions. In both instances, this true value is typically directed toward the reproduction and subsistence of the sources of capitalist value, such as labor, in order to compensate for the deficiencies inherent in capital's allocation (e.g., insufficient wages). Capital itself tends to return value solely for the reproduction of these sources as expendable entities (e.g., labor qua labor). However, these non-transformative types of true value are ultimately subsumed into capitalist value production if they do not lead to any lasting weakening or replacement of capitalist relations. The true value that could have been produced prior to capitalist decommonization represents 'the potential commonist true value lost' in the equation. When fundamental sources of true value are decommonized by capital, acknowledging the diminished potential for creating such value is crucial, even if quantifying its magnitude is challenging.

Fetish value is the product of interaction between the inner and outer organization of capital. *The outer organization of capital is the constantly shifting frontiers of capital where the annexation and decommonization of the sources of true value occurs, whereas the inner structure of capital is where the already decommonized sources of value are incorporated into the capitalist process of extracting capitalist surplus value* (see Figure 4.4).

As capital grows through decommonization, the magnitude of the true value lost in the outer organization of capital becomes greater than the magnitude of the capitalist value produced inside the inner organization, leading to a growingly negative magnitude of fetish value.

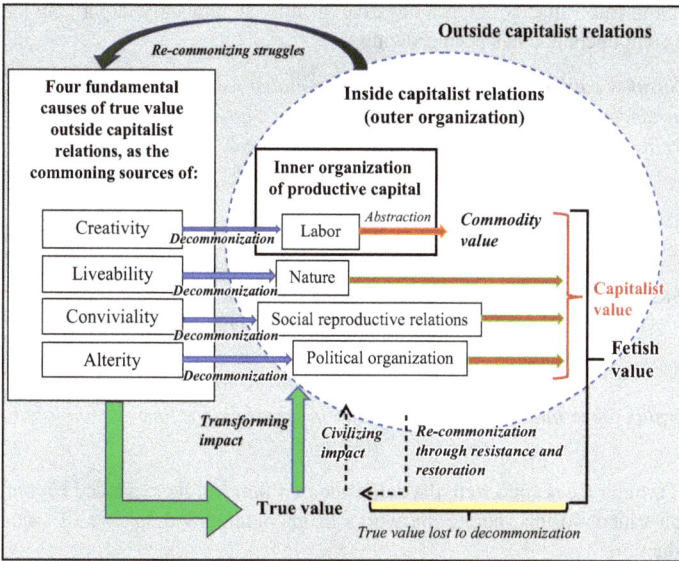

Figure 4.4 The inner and outer organizations of capital, inside and outside capitalist relations.

Fetish value = *aggregate capitalist value – capitalist value expended on the regeneration of the sources of capitalist value + deficit true value under capital*

Or

Fetish value = *[aggregate capitalist value – capitalist value expended on the regeneration of decommonized sources of capitalist value + true value produced inside the capitalist production relations] + [true value produced outside the capitalist production relations resulting in the endurance of existing commons subject to decommonization – true value consumed and expropriated by capital – true value lost to entropy – potential commonist true value lost to decommonization]*

The first three components within the first pair of brackets in the equation above constitute the net 'surplus capitalist value' and occur within the capitalist relations, including the inner structure of productive capital. Surplus capitalist value is then the difference between the aggregate capitalist value produced, and the capitalist value expended to regenerate its decommonized sources of value, which are alienated labor, nature, social reproduction, and capital's political organization. The second pair of brackets denotes the net deficit in true value, which is a negative quantity significantly larger than the first component and has been growing.

Surplus capitalist value = *aggregate capitalist value − capitalist value expended on the regeneration of the sources of capitalist value + true value produced inside the capitalist relations, but outside capitalist production relations*[4]

Originally, according to Marx, surplus value is the commodity value, originated from surplus labor. It is thus:

Surplus (commodity) value = *aggregate commodity value produced by labor − value of labor power*[5]

Or in other words:

Surplus labor time= *aggregate socially necessary labor time*[6] *− paid labor time*[7]

Through the second step, the definition of value will be expanded beyond surplus labor to incorporate the works of uncommodified spheres of value production.

The 'surplus capitalist' value is the sum of all surpluses extracted out of the reified forms of the four fundamental causes of value:

Surplus capitalist value = *aggregate capitalist value − capitalist value expended on the regeneration of the sources of capitalist value = surplus value extracted from labor + surplus value extracted from nature + surplus value extracted from social reproduction + surplus value extracted from political organization*

Surplus commodity value extracted from labor = *total human labor power expended − capitalist value expended on labor's reproduction*

Surplus capitalist ecological value extracted from ecosystems = *total ecosystem services (or nature's work) − capitalist value expended on maintaining, sustaining, and rehabilitating these services*

Surplus capitalist social value extracted from social reproduction = *total work of social reproduction resulting in the reproduction of labor and addressing the social, ecological, and political externalities of capital − capitalist value expended on the regeneration of social reproduction*

Surplus capitalist political value extracted from political organization = *total organizational work increasing aggregate capitalist value − capitalist value expended on the political organization of capital*

The scope of this volume does not allow for the comprehensive exploration of all major aspects of capitalist and commonist modes of value production using the modular framework developed here. That would require us to show how, under capital, the potential for the generation of true value out of and for each commons is distorted, how fetish value is instead constructed, how the localized/regionalized fetish value regimes, in turn, accelerate the decommonization process, how contentious stability is injected through civilizing meta-mechanisms, and how transformative praxes are possible and at work to restore and originate true value while displaying their complex (nondualist) relationships with capital. However, the next two chapters will begin this exploration by revisiting the Marxian labor theory of value and proposing ways to reconstruct it from the perspective of the commonist framework. Through engagement with post-Marxist and Marxian revisionist arguments, these chapters offer a platform to delve into the intricate and abstract concepts introduced earlier.

Notes

1 The differences between 'primary abstraction' and 'secondary abstraction' are delineated in more details in the next chapter. (See also Hosseini, 2022b).
2 The costs of climate inaction continue to grow exponentially. The slower and more inadequate the measures, the more burdensome they become. Numerous scientific reports, including the Stern Review in 2006 and the more recent IPCC reports, confirm that the costs of inaction on climate change are projected to be significantly higher than the costs of action.
3 Capital's 'political organization' or 'power structure,' as the bearer of capital's final cause, is the diffuse and pervasive force that regulates and structures social relations and economic systems in a way that privileges the interests of capital over other social and ecological concerns. This power operates through enchantment, e.g., the production and dissemination of knowledge, desires, norms, and ideologies that naturalize capitalist relations and structures, and make alternatives appear impossible or undesirable.
4 Examples of this are the reproductive work executed to sustain labor or the communal works expanded to addresses the ecological or social externalities of capital.
5 The value of labor power is the labor time socially necessary to produce the means of subsistence of workers 'as workers.'
6 Expended in the production of commodities.
7 Socially necessary to produce means of laborers' substance, as determined by competition in the labor market and through the private exchange of means of subsistence of value producers.

5 Toward a Commonist (Labor) Theory of Value

This chapter,[1] revisits and reconstructs the Marxian labor theory of value by drawing on the commonist framework outlined in the previous chapter. The focus here is on the commoning sources of creativity while staying mindful of the deep interconnections between all four fundamental commons sources of true value, as illustrated in Figure 2.1. It argues that 'labor' is an outcome of the decommonization of human (and by extension, more-than-human) creative power through the abstraction and appropriation of infra-processes. To avoid confusion between the abstraction infra-process – which results in the perversion of 'creativity' into 'productivity' or 'creative power' to 'labor power' – and the abstraction in Marxian theory, the chapter refers to the former as 'primary abstraction' and the latter as 'secondary abstraction' (see Figure 5.1).

Primary abstraction creates labor and labor power outside the inner organization of capitalist production relations where capital's socio-ecological frontiers are located. Whereas, secondary abstraction, as Marx theorized, results in the formation of abstract labor and productive capitalist value represented by exchange-value and surplus value within the inner organization of capital. This differentiation is critical in helping us avoid productivism both in our interpretation of Marxian value theory and in our post-capitalist alternatives. The chapter will expand on this dichotomy and discuss its potential for resolving major disagreements over the suitability of Marxian value theory in the context of so-called post-industrial capital.

The Lost Commoning Origin of Labor

The key assumption here is that human creativity, understood as a fundamental commons and the efficient cause of true value in the commonist state of living, is perverted into labor under capital. Labor then becomes a material cause (substance) of fetish value by losing its subjectivity as a result of being alienated from its commoning origin. This loss of subjectivity is due to the alienation of labor from its original commoning nature as human creativity, which existed in accord with extra-human creativity. In light of these claims, the question arises as to how well this postulation aligns with Marx's conception of the real abstraction of labor.

DOI: 10.4324/9781003340386-5

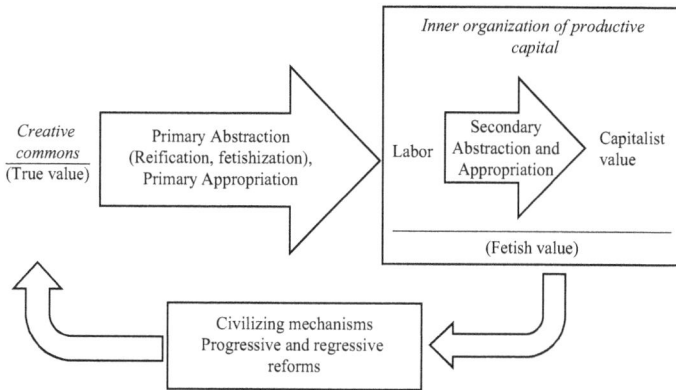

Figure 5.1 The perversion of human creative power as a commoning source of true value into labor as a source of capitalist value through the primary and secondary abstractions and appropriations.

Unpacking Marx's Notion of Labor

The description of the key categories of labor and production is not unproblematic in Marx's political–economic works (Pomeroy, 2004, p. 44). Marx moves back and forth between different levels of analysis, i.e., the general and the historically specific levels, and between pre-capitalist and capitalist modes of production, while using the same terms. This can cause confusion between the normative and analytical treatment of value. However, Marx (1990, p. 283) gives an indication of the issue:

> We shall, therefore, in the first place, have to consider the labour process independently of any specific social formation. Labour is, first of all, a process between man and nature; a process by which man, through his own actions, mediates, regulates, and controls the metabolism between himself and nature.

At this general level, Marx practically considers labor as an 'efficient cause' (using Aristotelian terminology) in shaping the present from the perspective of the future or telos, which is the communally determined good life (Hudis, 2019, p. 761). Marx views the 'use-value' of labor as a creative potential to fulfill genuine human desires and needs. Under capitalism, this natural use-value is distorted by being repurposed for generating surplus value fetishized from an exchange-value perspective (Foster, 2022).

Further expanding upon this logic requires distinguishing between two types of value: 'true value,' defined from the perspective of (more than) human genuine needs fulfillment, and 'fetish value,' defined from the non-fulfillment viewpoint (Hosseini, 2022a). Failing to make this distinction reduces 'true value' to the labor time necessary only for the reproduction of labor power, which mistakenly conflates the reproduction of commodified labor with the satisfaction of the genuine needs of laborers, their communities, and ecosystems. To address the challenges in Marx's analysis, we must carefully distinguish between distinct levels of analysis and use appropriate terms. By so doing, we can better understand the nature of labor and production in different social formations and develop a more nuanced understanding of value that reflects the primacy of fulfilling genuine human and ecological needs.

Marx describes labor in general as a 'human productive subjectivity' or a 'life-producing-life' activity through which humanity reproduces its existence through material interchange with the inorganic nature. It is a productive activity that is a 'mediation' where the unity of man and nature is established and humanity as a species-being is realized (Starosta, 2022, pp. 119–124). Human beings actualize their bodily vital powers through the conscious and transformative application of the productive powers of labor to satisfy their needs. These needs are not solely dictated by their physical nature but are also influenced by sophisticated intellectual and social factors. These factors, in turn, are shaped by the process of production and historically conditioned by modified or humanized natural environments. The product of human life activity (whose form already exists ideally in the actors' imagination at the beginning of the production process) will thus include both the material goods and services with useful material, symbolic, and/or affective effects. The satisfaction of such needs is essential for the reproduction and expansion of the creative powers of individuals and communities.

The immanent social character of human creative power at the general level, as 'affirmatively' highlighted by Marx in *Capital* and *Grundrisse*, implies the capacity of his value theory to envision the origin of labor as a commons. However, except in theoretical abstraction, there is no general level of human productive power that exists in isolation. Instead, it is embedded within social production relations rather than materialized in a vacuum. Labor that gives value to commodities is not transhistorical from Marx's perspective. It is only under capitalism that it appears to be a natural fact of life (Vitale, 2020). Therefore, there can be no transhistorical essence without roots in the evolutionary development of this original 'life-producing-life' capacity in human societies. It would be an ontologically baseless theoretical abstraction (and therefore a redundant argumentation) if we do not consider the real social formation – no matter how remotely imaginable or relatively historically primitive – that underpins the realization of human creative power in its *organic unity* with the community and the rest of nature. This unity is one in which human creative power not only produces life inclusive of itself but also draws inspiration from organized life. Thus, it will have no mechanical relationship with the commoning sources of liveability.

Part of this intrinsic indigeneity of the commoning nature of human creative power is an evolutionary product of the interactions between human beings as part of the life-domain. Therefore, we are here ultimately speaking about more-than-human and more-than-production creative power. This creative power has never been purely or fully realized in its perfect commons forms as it has been subject to historically formed hierarchical relations (even prior to the agricultural revolution). However, due to such historical rootedness in reality and relative presence in commoning relations, it is always possible for humans to futuristically develop social formations under which the indigenous essence of the creative power as a fundamental commons is emancipated and almost fully actualized.

The True Value of (More Than) Human Creative Power as an Essential Commons

To avoid confusion and in accordance with the suggested differentiation between true value and fetish value, the use of word 'labor' is proposed to be restricted to instances when it is exercised under the capitalist social formation. Instead, the more general term 'creative power' (of which 'unalienated work'[2] is one form) is employed when considering it in a general context or presupposing it under the commonist state of living. In the commonist state of living, any value extracted is mutually compensated with (counter-)value injected, so the commons and the relationships between them would persist. Marx was aware of the importance of the distinction between the so-called general and specific levels and attributed the confusion between them to the bourgeois political economy, which results in naturalizing/de-historicizing capitalist relations. However, this distinction is not translated into terminological precision in his value theory.

Marx's LTV can be reconstructed in a few ways by drawing on the idea of 'commoning.' The concept of 'commoning' usually refers to the social process of creating and managing commons, which are shared resources held in common and managed by a community. Marx's value theory is unique in emphasizing the social relations of value creation, including the role of capital and labor in the production process. By drawing on the idea of commoning, we can see that this socially necessary labor time includes not only the time required to produce the commodity but also the time required to manage and maintain the commons on which the production depends. Thus, *the value of a commodity is not determined only by individual labor but also by the social (reproductive) relations of commoning that sustain the production process.*

According to the commonist perspective, human creative power is a fundamental commons interactively woven into the fabric of the commoning sources of liveability. When appearing in its unalienated form and essence, it strives to create a future where the flourishing of all life becomes a genuine historical possibility. Therefore, by efficiently organizing and orchestrating socio-ecological production relations under the commonist state of living, human creative power plays a crucial role in realizing the telos of true value. Recently, the concept of 'labor as commons' has gained traction among transformative scholars and activists in the global North (Azzellini, 2016). This new theoretical tendency is not surprising, considering the recent resurgence of the idea of commons/commoning, the rise of digital modes of production, widespread corporate extraction of value out of digital commons in knowledge forms, and the growing movements for worker-owned companies and protecting natural commons and the Indigenization of post-capitalist discourses in the global North. Additionally, there have been indigenous struggles to defend their lands and other natural resources in the global South, as well as the anti-privatization movements inspired by the struggle for re-communalizing privatized public services and reclaiming urban public spaces.

Highlighting the commoning aspect of labor, despite being in an embryonic stage, is a useful step forward. However, we cannot establish such a postulation about the nature of labor simply by accentuating the social and cooperative characteristics of individuals' capabilities to produce within capitalist production relations. Doing so would only address the 'formal cause' of labor after it has been decommonized by capital while failing to take into account the other three aspects: the efficient, the material, and the final causes of capitalist value. Furthermore, productive labor has already lost its commoning essence by entering into capitalist commodity production relations.

Beyond Reductionist Notions of Commons and Commoning

The idea of commons as spaces independent from private ownership and state control potentially poses a challenge to the ideological dualism of market fundamentalism versus state centrism inherited from the Cold War. As a discourse to frame transformative praxis, commons can rejuvenate progressive responses to both neoliberalism and the potential return of statism (state-controlled capitalism, state capitalism, or state socialism). However, there are already two major ways of conceptualizing commons that impair transformative capacity. These are not mutually exclusive. The first one limits the scope of commons to social relations shaped around natural or artificial common resources. This is not only popular among institutionalists like Elinor Ostrom (2015) but also among many Marxist and eco-socialist theorists, resulting in the treatment of commons as the objects of human actions[3] and thus dis-integrating the economic from the ecological.

The second is the perception of commons as shared 'ownership' rather than 'stewardship' and 'right to govern.' This reduces it to the third segment of the economy (the so-called shared, peer-to-peer, open-access) in parallel with the public and private sectors. Being a sector alongside the public and private is, at best, a negation of only the extreme ideological perspectives (e.g., neoliberalism and statism). These approaches run the risk of making the idea less transformative and susceptible to being incorporated into the civilizing meta-mechanisms of capital.[4] Replacing capitalist 'accumulation-by-dispossession' with 'accumulation-by-cooption' is not meaningfully progressive.[5] Therefore, it is the negation of this negation that is emancipatory, and the notional expansion of commons becomes an ontological base for the post-capital emancipatory praxes and a normative/axiological base for defining value.

Commons encompass more than just tangible entities such as common-pool resources, public spaces, shared ownership, or commonwealth institutions. To avoid reductionism in understanding commons and commoning, the Aristotelian theory of causation can be used. By applying the four causes to the concept of commons, a more nuanced and comprehensive understanding can be obtained that recognizes the multiple dimensions and levels of commons and commoning. This includes the agential, ecological, and social structural, as well as the iterative processes through which they are sustained and regenerated.

A commons is a living ecosystem, or a complex 'species-being' in and of itself, which – according to the Aristotelian doctrine of causality – consists of four constituting elements. Firstly, the efficient cause is the activities of the commoners (both human and non-human) and their subjectivities, which include skills, knowledge, agency, experiences, and capabilities that are actualized through the process of building and maintaining commons, as well as their 'organs as tools' and 'tools as organs.'[6] Secondly, the material cause is a set of resources that are held in common, conserved, enhanced, and governed collectively, as well as the flows of energy and mass in and out of the commons as an open system. Thirdly, the formal cause is its structure, or what Marx would refer to as an 'ensemble of social [ecological] relations,' along with their corresponding forms of cooperation and conviviality across a plurality of subjects, as well as the norms, rules, evaluative measures, and mutual rights and responsibilities that regulate these relations and guide actions toward the realization of the final cause. Finally, the final cause is the self-sustaining and life-regenerating function of the commons as a living being seeking a good life through the transformative praxis of commoning by the commoners (De Angelis, 2022; Mau, 2022).

A redefined notion of commons, informed by the Aristotelian theory of causation, could provide several benefits when applied to understanding the nature of human creative power. Human creative power (or labor in a general or free sense) can be considered as commons consisting of the four elements described above. Its efficient cause is rooted in the reproductive work that takes place in households and communities. Human creative power is organized and sustained within the care and community-based *oikos(es)*, with recognition given to the true value of all forms of creative power in contributing to more-than-human well-living. However, when human creative power is subsumed under capitalist production relations, it is the capitalist class that takes on the efficient role, controlling the labor process through the hiring and firing of workers, setting wages and working conditions, and using technology and resources to extract surplus value.

The material cause of human creative power is comprised of the physiological concreteness of bodily features and organs, the matter–energy bodily metabolism, and the intellect-affective capacities for creativity and productivity at both the individual and collective levels. These elements constantly contribute to and are regenerated in a healthy commonist state of living. This is in contrast to the physical or use-value of labor performed solely to produce capitalist value.

The formal cause of human creative power as a commons encompasses the interconnectedness of bodily organs and the microbiome, as well as the social interconnectedness and solidarity based on the principles of reciprocity, mutual aid, and cooperation among all value producers, including non-human beings. This social form recognizes the interdependence of human and non-human creativity and prioritizes the well-being of people and the environment over the accumulation of capital. Inherent to the activity of commoning is the eroding of distinctions between the ruled and the ruler, which transcends the capitalist disintegration between the social and political aspects of commoning. This contrasts with the formal cause of value under capitalism, which involves the formal organization of labor, including the division of labor, the hierarchy of management and labor, and the legal and institutional frameworks that regulate labor relations, all of which are characterized by the exploitation of labor to generate profit.

The final cause of human creative power as a commons is the commonist state of (more-than-human) living-well-together, which serves as both a commoning praxis and a project of commoning. This is the driving force behind the activities that prioritize the creation of true value for the benefit of the commoners over increasing productivity, reducing labor costs, and expanding markets, all in pursuit of greater profits as the capitalist final cause of production.

The praxis of commoning that ensures the endurance of the commons is not an unexciting repetitive struggle for the mere sake of survival through a universal commitment to a simple mass-energy balance principle. Rather, it is an act of *alterity*, or constant reinvention of the self and surroundings, with partly unexpected results, conditioned with and in response to a continually changing environment. Existential causality should be seen as an evolutionary-iterative transitional process rather than a conjunction of events. This means that a commons is both an entity (although with fuzzy contours) and an evolutionary process through which the final cause acts as a dynamic determinant by reorganizing the process in its own ultimate image.

The flows of energy and mass in and out of each commons (or, in fact, between them) make it physically impossible for a commons to be a self-sufficient closed system. In the life-domain, commons are deeply intertwined and radically entangled with one another. This means that every commons cannot function properly as a commons if its connection in the network of interdependent commons is disrupted or if the other associated commons are decommonized. Human creative power as a commons is interdependent and intertwined with other commons in the life-domain. Under capitalism, social norms, historical traditions, and ecological contexts shape human creativity and innovation. However, capitalist production relations disrupt and also sever these cross-commons entanglements. Human creativity's causal power as a source of value is undermined and perverted to a mere means of production and profit.

The causal power of an object is intrinsic to its structure, and therefore, with a change in the object's structure, the nature of its causal power also changes (Harré & Madden, 1975). The structure of concrete creative power as a commons, which is its concreteness, is its material cause. *This gives it the causal power to function as an autonomous efficient cause of true value independent of capitalist relations.* Under capital's rule, labor is reified primarily, leading to a change in its structure, and its causal power as a potential efficient cause of value (in the form of work) transforms into a material cause in the process of commodity production (material and/or immaterial). This material cause can be directly exploited as the so-called productive labor, turned into a substance of value, and/or be expropriated as the so-called non-productive labor, a gift of (human) nature from which value is extracted.

Labor is the product of the decommonization of human creativity and its alienation from its original commoning nature, which continues in the capitalist commodity production process through the secondary abstraction process (theorized by Marx). *What defines labor as labor (productive or unproductive from capital's point of view) is the 'primary abstraction' process.*

The unique ability of labor to produce value-added cannot be its only defining feature. Marx explains that even outside capitalist relations, 'surplus work' is normally needed. For Marx, the imagined post-capitalist "association of free and equal producers" who own the means of production in common and expend "their many different forms of labor power in full self-awareness" would still need to conduct surplus labor to maintain and upgrade their means of production and to meet the various needs of the society where the association comes from and the association's own needs as a communal being (Marx, 1990, pp. 171–172). Private exchange no longer determines the value, and thus, no fetishization of commodities happens. Hence, in this situation, according to Marx, the social relations of producers will be simple and transparent in all moments. Marx assumes, "only for the sake of a parallel with the production of commodities," that the "labor time" necessary to produce use-value would still need to be employed to determine the contribution of each worker and to finely apportion, through social planning, the right magnitudes of appropriate labor functionalities to produce for the satisfaction of various collective needs.

The Roots of Alienation: The Loss of Commoning Origin and Nature

In the world of contingencies, every cause has a cause. Labor as a cause of value is also caused. Once again, from the Aristotelian perspective of causality, labor must have four types of causes, all subject to decommonization under capitalism. In other words, labor, to be possessed by capital, has to be 'dispossessed' of its causal structure. For this to happen, capital, through the secondary abstraction process, has to decommonize the four constituting elements of labor: (1) its material cause, which is its concreteness; (2) its efficient cause, which is its life activity or what reproduces labor; (3) its formal cause, or the communal cohesion and solidarity among the value producers; and (4) its final cause, which is its function to prefiguratively fulfill needs, create meaningful and gratifying living experiences, and advance collective well-living. These four types of appropriation of the commoning features of labor, respectively, correspond to the four types of alienation of laboring individuals that Marx specifically theorized: Alienation as the estrangement of workers (1) from their own essential species-being; (2) from their life activity; (3) from one another; and (4) from the product of their labor.

By understanding the correspondence between the four types of alienation and the four Aristotelian causes of labor, we can see how the process of decommonization under capitalism has resulted in the fragmentation and subjugation of labor as a common resource. The dehumanizing effects of capitalism can be seen in the way that workers are reduced to mere instruments of production, and their labor is stripped of its communal, creative, and prefigurative potential.

The efficient cause of labor is the life-making work of *oikos* that, under capital is perverted into unwaged social reproductive labor. However, unlike productive labor, reproductive work is not directly capitalized through secondary abstraction. Rather, it is only primarily abstracted and expropriated alongside the rest of nature. This way, like unpaid surplus wage labor, unwaged social reproductive labor loses its creative subjectivity and becomes a material cause for the reproduction of so-called productive labor, instead of being an efficient cause alongside creative work *in the commoning process of true value production*. The unwaged reproductive laborer receives a portion of the wage (assuming the household relations are fair), won by the breadwinner in exchange for their contribution to the reproduction of labor and, by extension, of fetish value, and this way, it becomes reified (deprived of their subjectivity) but not commodified (unless waged directly by working, for example as a care worker).

The material cause of labor is its concreteness – its natural bodily and mental power for creativity and the socially produced embedded skills and knowledge, which are the by-products of the metabolic interaction with the rest of nature through social reproduction. The alienation of labor from the rest of nature turns labor into a mere tool, a biological machine, alienated from its life activity.

Care, when exercised in non-alienating relations among value producers, is the backbone of conviviality, which is the formal cause of true value in the commonist social formation. However, with the decommonization of convivial sources of true value, care is reduced to a range of institutionalized qualities, from the so-called 'positive culture' of collegiality to 'compassionate leadership' to staff well-being programs and a whole range of performative gestures of corporate social responsibility; only simulated care that masks the exploitation inherent in the capitalist mode of production, perpetuating the illusion of a compassionate work environment while preserving the power dynamics and inequalities that underpin it.

Counter-management comradeship and solidarity among worker union members, where there is no agenda to restore the commoning nature of care and conviviality, appear as part of a countermovement to the social disembeddedness of the economy. However, without a transformative vision that challenges the underlying power structures and aims to reinstate genuine care and conviviality, such initiatives can only provide temporary relief within the confines of the existing capitalist framework.

The communal settings of value producers outside their workplaces, as another aspect of the commoning formal cause of their labor, also need to change for the causal structure of labor to change (from efficient cause to material cause of fetish value). The conviviality of communal support that gives workers their communal existence turns into social relations between commodities produced by labor, mediated by the market, and governed by the exogenous forces of politics, thus losing its convivial essence. Labor, therefore, loses its convivial solidarity base and becomes socially alienated from its internal and broader communities. The reification of human relations under capital has to be complemented with commodity-money relations fetishized as a (pseudo-)community, thus giving a false sense of living in a commons built around self-seeking or hedonistic relationships between the participants.

The final cause in the employment of human creative power is originally its prefigurative function to transcend the status quo and achieve a higher level of communal well-living and self-thriving through alterity. However, it has been replaced with the regeneration of capitalist and fetish value, which is commodified or contained in the products of labor. This results in the alienation of producers from the outcomes of their activities.

The problem of alienation within production relations is not rooted in the replacement or subjugation of use-value by exchange-value but rather in their contradictory duality. Alienation extends beyond commodity production relations and begins when human creativity through primary abstraction that perverts it into labor loses its capacity to function as an efficient commoning source of true value. Capital as an object gains subjectivity and the status of an active self-energizing final cause. Therefore, not only commodity exchanges guided by social value complexes abstract human creativity (by inverting its subjective and objective aspects) but also the decommonized sources of alterity (such as the capitalist legal, political, and cultural regimes) determine the terms of exchange and regulations, as the formal cause granting capital an autocratic control over the entire process.

The laborers become alienated not only from their labor (products and processes of production) but also from their convivial life (solidarity with other laborers and their own broader communities), from the rest of nature, and from their collective self-determining power (as an open-ended final cause). *Alienation should, therefore, not be seen simply as a side-effect of capitalist production relations but also as an imperative factor in the entire capitalization process rooted in the decommonization of the life-domain.*

To liberate labor, it is far from adequate to merely struggle to restore its capacity for healthy self-reproduction as labor. Granting laborers ownership of the means of production does not restore the concreteness of their creative power if the realization of the value they produce is still subject to private exchanges. Even if the buyers and sellers of labor power are the same groups of producers, their labor is still subject to abstraction and commodification (i.e., "capitalism without capitalists"). The true liberation of laborers will require commonizing their labor back into more-than-human creativity, which itself requires (re-)commonizing their material, efficient, formal, and final causes of existence.

In other words, labor can achieve its full commoning status only when the broader context in which production processes function is also commonized. This includes political institutions, community relations, ownership, cultural complexes, labor and commodity markets, and more (see the next section). *Disentangling our lives from both state and market by creating autonomous spaces of commoning does not necessarily lead to the full realization of the commonist state of being unless the state and the market, as well as their underpinning value systems, are profoundly reshaped in the image of commons.*[7] The concept of commons should be expanded beyond its traditional scope to include also the complex web of social, economic, and political relations within and between markets, states, and their entangled ecological and cultural systems (Gills & Hosseini, 2022).

Azzellini's (2016, p. 772) study of worker-recuperated companies (WRCs) in Latin America reveals their strengths and their limitations. Self-organizing communities are built, new values and norms based on solidarity and conviviality emerge, and the metabolic relationship with the sources of liveability may positively change as the purpose of production shifts more toward the reproduction of what is essential for the communal life. The results radiate beyond the contours of such commoning praxes with potentially strong implications for the community economy and even for wider politics. However, their linkages with the capitalist state and market continue to be unproductive at best, and the disintegration between production and reproduction activities remains almost the same. Such examples, at most, more closely resemble common source pool institutions that are the center of new institutionalist attention than the necessary means of a social revolution.[8] For the latter to happen, a paradigmatic shift is required. A commonist theory of value must be very attentive to the relationships between commons and capital (De Angelis, 2022, p. 651).

The Unheeded Primary Abstraction

The commonist theory of value requires us to differentiate between primary and secondary abstractions of labor. As defined earlier, abstraction is the inversion between the subject and the object, i.e., reification complemented with fetishization. In this sense, both primary and secondary types of abstraction have the same essence. However, it is their location that makes them different. Marx theorized the (secondary) abstraction (of commodified/wage labor) within/through the inner organization of capital. Primary abstraction (see Figures 4.1 and 5.1) consists of the reification and fetishization of the fundamental commons; in this case, the (more-than-human) commoning sources of creativity. Primary abstraction is independent of capitalist formats (the industrial versus the post-industrial, the Fordist versus the post-Fordist, etc.). It is what labor (commodified or not) is born out of. In fact, primary abstraction has become more prominent in the 'late capitalism' of advanced economies since capital has constantly developed effective ways of extracting fetish value out of uncommodified-yet-reified work such as care, social, and ecological services.

But for concrete labor to be subsumed into abstract labor (which is no longer capable of producing true value) and for commodities to become the bearer of exchange-value (which can be converted into prices), specific social relationships must have already emerged and been sustained as preconditions for the constant reemergence of labor. This specific form of production relations is characterized by the separation of the objective conditions of production (means of production) and the subjective conditions (labor power). This separation results in the bifurcation of labor itself (concrete and abstract) and the bifurcation of value. This separation is both the product and the producer of a *decommonized society* (in Marx's narrower term, the 'commodity society'), which transcends the inner organization of capital and underpins its persistence. It is a society in which the fundamental sources of creativity, liveability, conviviality, and alterity are constantly perverted into abstract labor, objectified nature, alienating hierarchical relations, and self-fossilizing political cultures, respectively.

For Marx, abstract labor is the substance (or material cause) of capitalist value. The more labor is (secondarily) abstracted, the more capitalist value is produced. Such abstraction, for Marx, is determined by the social average of labor time necessary for production, which is outside the workers' control. Abstraction makes the quantification of labor power, and thus its exchange, possible. However, a deeper investigation of the complexity of Marx's value theory paves the way to addressing its constraints using his own method.

According to Marx, the abstraction of labor depends on the exchange of the products of labor, which in one cycle happens after labor is already employed. Exchange is, therefore, a formal cause of abstraction. But how can exchange play such a role as a determinant of value? Exchange (inclusive of the exchanges of labor as a commodity) has a tacit political dimension since it is influenced by power relations, flows of information, and wealth distributions that constantly change. Hence, it constantly requires the actors involved to draw on their prefigurative capacities to speculate on the fluctuations in demands, supplies, costs, and prices, with ever 'imperfect' market information.

The secondary abstraction of labor via commodity exchanges is dependent on and deeply intertwined with the perversion of communal interdependences and actors' deliberative power to prefigure their communal futures into market relations and self-centered speculative actions in pursuit of profit.

Final causes operate through evolutionary processes, allowing them to influence the inputs of following circuits despite being the outputs of a previous causal process, giving the appearance of a teleological effect. In the case of social causal mechanisms in open systems, primitive bearers of the final cause coexist with and guide the other three fundamental causes from the outset of the process. These primitive bearers can emerge as cognitive–affective prefigurative tendencies, such as the desires, imaginations, and ideals of actors, as well as pre-established social institutions, like the so-called free markets and the state, which regulate social relations. As Marx theorized, in a society dominated by industrial capital, (capitalist) "value, as a representation of socially necessary abstract labor time ... imposes its finality and constraints on society as a whole" (Ouellet, 2015, p. 22).

Competitive private exchange serves a much deeper function beyond abstracting labor and making commodities (including labor) commensurable. It is a constantly recurring meta-mechanism that reshapes the values, desires, wants, and needs of actors, as well as their social institutional manifestations, in the image of the ultimate form of the final cause: capital. As a result, a secondary inversion of the subject and object occurs.

Marx (1989, pp. 544–545) later modified his view by considering 'exchange-value' as a mere "form of expression" of 'value' (as the content) and by clarifying that "commodity is both a use-value and value" (rather than use-value and exchange-value as opposites). It is possible to produce use-value and value without producing commodities. To produce a commodity, the use-value should be produced for others outside the proximate community of producers, i.e., social use-value, rather than for the community of producers (who may also exchange their products across their communities).

Marx addresses 'primary abstraction' by discussing the conversion from primitive modes of production to the capitalist mode of production through which the communal character of general labor is lost to the fetishized exchange of commodities. For Marx, in primitive production, the social character of the use-value of common products lies in their "communal character" rather than in their communal exchanges. For products to enter the world of commodities, they need to be produced under an economic formation through which the value of products assumes a form of expression distinct/independent from its natural form contained in the commodity. Thus, *the unity of value and use-value becomes a duality that translates itself into the dual character of labor, i.e., the useful/concrete form that produces use-value and the abstract form as the expenditure of labor power.*

Marx distinguishes between labor and labor power. In contrast to a slave society where masters own and control both the worker's body and capacity to work (i.e., the substantial and the efficient constituents of labor), in capitalism, it is only the capacity to work (i.e., labor power) that is being bought and sold as a commodity. The workers' bodies and the substance of their labor, and thus their subjectivity, remain free from full submission and objectification, unlike in slavery or serfdom (Hudis, 2019). The abstraction and commodification of labor is only a change in the form of labor power rather than in its content/substance.

The bifurcation between labor and labor power constitutes a potential for resistance. Under capital, and unlike abstract labor which functions as a material cause, concrete labor remains the mover and the efficient cause of value production, even if its role is systematically denied by capital through the laws of private exchange. The essence of labor (human creativity) remains a potential commons subject to constant decommonization, but also a potential source for the emergence of progressive alternatives to capital. However, the actualization of this potentiality is contingent upon a negation at a deeper level, which is *the negation of the infra-processes through which labor is constructed out of the decommonization of human creativity.*

The abolition of productive capitalist value, by negating the exchange-value, which is only an alienated expression of value, requires the abolition of the (secondarily) abstracted labor that is the substance of capitalist value. However, it would be a mistake to assume that the emancipation of labor and thus the working class ends here. Using the commonist value theory, we must extend this logic by acknowledging that the abolition of abstract labor is impractical as long as we still have an infra-process in place through which labor is primarily abstracted out of commoning sources of creativity. Labor, insofar as it functions as a material bearer of exchange-value, cannot be organized as a commoning praxis (Azzellini, 2016, p. 766). Therefore, *the full and meaningful liberation of laborers happens when the primary abstraction of labor is abolished, and labor as productive work is returned to its commoning status* as part of a wider, more-than-human capacity for creativity.

The secondary abstraction of labor within the inner organization of capital through the competitive private exchange, as theorized by Marx, is not possible without decommonizing the communal bonds between (more-than-human) producers of true value and the conversion into alienating commodity exchanges. The secondary abstraction is, in fact, the alteration of the formal aspect of the causal structure of labor (via the replacement of communal relations with private exchange) and thus is the further extension of primary abstraction into the inner organization of commodity production. 'Private exchange' is the perverted or decommonized version of convivial relations that functions as a formal cause by giving structure to the realization of the fetish value through the secondary abstraction of labor.

As Marx explains, exchange is a form of the socialization of labor. However, not every socialization of labor is part of its abstraction. For instance, labor was socialized but not abstracted in feudal society where the means of production were commonly shared. Secondary abstraction of labor becomes possible when this socialization happens through the means of private exchanges of the products of wage labor. Capital abstracts labor by perverting it from a potentially efficient and active cause of use-value into a material cause. The purpose is to turn labor into the bearer of its final cause (capitalist fetish value). This is possible through a mixture of privatized exchange structures and state intrusions that function as the formal cause of capitalist value. It happens when conviviality in a commonist state of sociality has already been, to an adequate degree, perverted into a 'commodity society' that forms the social bases of exchange and thus functions as a formal cause of fetish value. *A society dispossessed of its conviviality is deeply prone to the reconstruction of patriarchal and racial relations in modern forms.* Capital, in fact, cannot function effectively in the presence of commonist conviviality.

For capital to function as the 'final cause' of the abstraction of labor, it needs to concurrently transmute/pervert other fundamental commoning sources of true value (i.e., sources of conviviality/care, liveability, and alterity). Capital can never be indifferent to inequalities outside the realm of its so-called productive relations. The social substance of human *creativity* (work) is perverted into abstract labor deprived of agency and its potentiality for creating true value. It becomes a material cause of fetish value by being contained in commodities. As Engels emphasizes in his *Anti-Dühring* (1947, Part II, Chapter 6), Marx was the first to demonstrate that (under capital), "labour can have no value," since (capitalist) "value itself is nothing else than the expression of socially necessary human labour materialised in an object." However, a commonist perspective builds upon this postulate by highlighting that labor, in its participation within the capitalist system, becomes a tool of capital and contributes to the ongoing process of decommonizing the four fundamental sources of true value.

The private exchange under capital is also an abstracted (reified + fetishized) form of relationship with the 'natural resources' necessary for the production and reproduction of commodities, capital, and labor. Exchange, therefore, determines not only the abstraction of labor but also the abstraction of the so-called natural resources, by perverting the fundamental sources of *liveability* into reified entities whose prices are determined in markets. The conviviality of more-than-human reproductive relations is perverted into private exchange relations deprived of morality, empathy, and diversity to function as a formal cause, and the sources of *liveability* are perverted/objectified into the so-called natural resources (nature's free gifts) deprived of their intrinsic values and their subjectivities that enable them to regenerate and sustain themselves. Finally, the prefigurative power of humanity for alterity is converted to instrumentalist behaviors conservative enough to endure the will/power of capital. What is happening here is not simply an extraction of surplus value out of (surplus) labor but rather *the conversion of 'true value' as a 'real potentiality,' to 'fetish value' as a 'faked actuality' by simultaneously perverting all the four fundamental commons of organized life.*

Secondary Abstraction: The Primary Abstraction by Other Means

A deeper understanding of Marx's method reveals that (real) abstraction involves the inversion of subjective and objective aspects of a fundamental cause of value, such as human creativity. This is made possible through the fusion of two opposite mechanisms: reification and fetishization, which complement each other. Reification involves the conversion of a social subject or subjective aspect of a socio-ecological entity, such as private labor according to Marx in *Capital*, into an object, such as variable commodity capital. When employed at surplus levels, this can produce surplus value, which is the origin of profit. Despite the complexities of the 'transformation problem,' a 'labor theory of value' (LTV) can still explain quantitative exploitation. In contrast, fetishization is a process where an object, such as a product of labor, is given the status of a subject, such as commodities with the agency to determine the value of labor through a private exchange. Here, Marx's theory offers a "value theory of labor" (VTL), which was lacking in the works of his predecessors (Elson, 1979).

The two processes of reification and fetishization complement each other to bifurcate work into abstract and concrete labor. The subjectivity derived from concrete labor is assigned to its products, including the profit that is reinvested in production to reproduce capital, by giving them a determining power over ex-subjects (concrete labor) through exchange relations (realization of value in the commodity market and the reemployment of labor as a commodity in the labor market). *Real abstraction is thus an inversion of the subjective and objective aspects of a common resource, which results in its perversion from a source of true value to a source of fetish value.* This construction of the Marxian idea of real abstraction provides a broader analytical framework that is equally applicable to all other types of causal sources of true value.

Under a capitalist social formation, capital seizes the subjectivity and evaluative power of more-than-human agents of creativity,[9] reducing their efficient causality in value production to a mere material cause devoid of communal prefigurative power. More consciously and conscientiously than other species, humans have the capacity to use their evaluative–subjective power to envision a future and prefiguratively translate their perceptions of 'good life' (as the final cause) into their practices of true value creation. Under capital, however, their evaluative power and thus their efficient causal functions are reduced to their roles as self-centered atomized beings who have internalized the well-being of capital as their own. This feature of capital creates a hyper-reality[10] in contradiction with the reality of life since what underpins life as a commons is fundamentally different from the living conditions forged by capital.

The focus of the commonist value theory is not merely the transformation of value into price or any other value form of labor products or the correspondence between them.[11] Instead, it should be the perversion of the commoning sources of creativity into mere instruments for capitalist fetish value production. This perversion turns human creativity into a reified object, i.e., labor, with its dual functionality (concrete and abstract) emerging from commodity production and private exchange and being appropriated by capital in the money form of value.

The perversion of human creativity is indeed a 'trans-mutation' (transition in essence) rather than a 'trans-formation' (transition in form/quiddity/appearance/expression). What matters most is not the transformation of one value form to another but the substantial rift between the types of value that essentialize human creativity free from capital, as opposed to its perverted version (i.e., labor) under capital. After the perversion, capital can extract what it claims to be of 'value' by fetishizing it as (1) an allegedly naturally occurring utility worth exchanging at a certain market price, which is another perverted commons (i.e., the otherwise convivial communal interactions reconstructed in the form of private exchanges) supposedly promoting the well-being of 'consumer society' whose needs, values, desires, and wants are altered to play roles in realizing capital's final cause; (2) a legitimate necessity for the social conditions of the possibility of labor, by virtue of the use-value embodied in the means of subsistence; (3) a fetishized right crystallized in the form of 'wage' that purports to represent the value of work expended; and finally, (4) a means to meet the imperatives of capital's reproduction (reinvestment in variable and constant capital) necessary for sustaining the whole system, into which labor, as capital's Other, is co-opted.

Marx in *Capital* is well aware of perversion but does not expand the scope of his value theory to include it, for the reasons we explained earlier. It is true that the complexity of his value theory has been largely overshadowed by the dominance of the interpretations that consider his work as an extension of the classical legacies (i.e., the 'labor theory of value') (Riva, 2022). The point of departure in the analysis of labor should be shifted to the normative commonist state of living, where human labor exists in the form of its unreified essence. This is not contrary to Marx's method. As Dobb (1972) argued in his interpretation of *Capital*, the starting point for Marx, contra the conventional interpretations, is not the commensurability of commodities due to their contained abstract labor. Rather, Marx starts from before the doubling of the product of labor happens, where the turning of objects of utility (i.e., natural and social forms of wealth) into commodities becomes possible through the private and autonomous processes of valorization (Riva, 2022).

The reification of human creativity into labor power, and then its further reification into abstract labor, has to be complemented by its fetishization for the secondary abstraction to become complete. Wage labor is fetishized and sanctified in the name of 'work,' as the only way for the majority to meet their needs and reclaim their dignity (Gorz, 1999). From family values to school curriculums, from welfare policies to social security, public healthcare, and social work, and from prison systems to military services, all are mobilized to create work-ready subjects (Weeks, 2011, pp. 6–7). This requires social institutions to be restructured away from their commoning nature, through their modernization. Their institutionalization under modernity is the infra-process through which they become the apparatus for the decommonization of creative power and the bearers of the mechanisms for 'civilizing' capital.

Only a fetishized form of value, extracted out of a reified commons, i.e., more-than-human creative power, can be translated into prices and profits, as they are now of the same essence. Thus, in this alienating environment, the owners/sellers of labor as a commodity internalize the imperatives of living under capital. According to these imperatives, (1) their prefigurative struggles should aim at gaining parity with capital and thus reducing their relative Otherness and (2) treating the impedimental consequences of capitalist production for the survival of the subaltern Other, such as non-human living beings, reproductive labor, marginalized communities, the indigenous, the immigrant, the colonized, the racialized, and the like, as externalities, improves living standards by making the social reproduction of both labor and capital more economically viable.

The magnitude of the value of labor congealed as 'socially necessary labor time' is determined by commodities in private exchange processes. Abstraction of labor in *Capital* is the byproduct of the unity of production and circulation. The valorization process (extraction of value out of labor) ultimately yields no value from capital's point of view if the realization processes fail. If there is no utility in the commodity made for others, there will be no value, and therefore, the employed labor does not count as productive. But what defines and determines utility? Indeed, commodities (material and immaterial) are not merely produced for the sake of being exchanged. Although exchange-value subsumes use-value, the latter remains critical. Use-value is not simply the physical qualities of the products of labor (Bellofiore, 2018). It is more importantly shaped by the consumerist society's socio-ideologically manufactured perceptions of utility, influenced by social preferences. These are themselves the societal manifestations of culturally constructed wants, desires, values, and needs of the populace. The so-called superstructure, here the societal interactions that construct preferences, plays a decisive role in the production of value in the base. The superstructure, as part of the formal cause, becomes an inducer of fetish value (the final cause) in the abstraction of proletarianized labor.

The value/want/desire/need complexes of a society under a commonist state of living (i.e., webs of daily socio-ecological interactions guided by convivial norms and values, oriented toward a communal imagination of a more-than-human good life) are fundamental social commons by nature that provide human creativity with the formal causes it needs to generate true value as the essence of the good life, i.e., its final cause. If these causal sources of conviviality could maintain their commoning nature (as an association of free actors living in a commonist state of being), the quantity, quality, utility, and worth of the products would be decided freely to favor the well-living of the given more-than-human community, rather than to satisfy the private profit motive. Therefore, capital depends on de-commonizing the commoning sources of alterity into modern state and political institutions that idealize and rationalize (mainly) those (innovative) actions that are oriented toward the endless accumulation of capitalist value.

In sum, after applying the above reconstructed Marxian logic to a scope broader than the inner dynamism of productive labor, we can infer that the *secondary abstraction of labor power is not only made possible, by but also is the extension of, primary abstraction infra-process through which human creativity, as an 'efficient' fundamental cause of true value, is trans-muted into a reified-fetishized-appropriated, de-essentialized object called 'labor' deprived of its organic connections with the other three fundamental commons.* Labor is born out of such a primary abstraction (*reification + fetishization*) of human creativity, a decommonizing infra-process, and thus is ready to be translated into a commodity form, that commodity value that can be extracted and appropriated by capital. What Marx calls 'abstract labor' captures this process only within the inner structure of capital where human creativity is already perverted into labor.

For Marx, abstract labor is a process of value creation as the result of making diverse concrete labor commensurable under the disciplinary force of competition (Blackledge, 2015). But, even within this limited realm of productive capital, it is not simply the proportionality of the rate of exploitation and rate of surplus value extraction – assuming that proportionality can finally be substantiated in the terrain of mathematical discourse – that discloses the nature of exploitation (Bellofiore & Coveri, 2022). Marx in *Capital* attributes the qualitative aspect (nature) of exploitation to the essential change in labor vis-à-vis capital; "*Abstraction and exploitation become virtually co-extensive … at the stage of the 'real subsumption of labour to capital*" (2022, p. 184, emphasis from original).

Labor is primarily a product of primary abstraction, subject to further de-essentialization under secondary abstraction when directly engaged in commodity production. However, labor does not necessarily need to go through the secondary abstraction process to become the provider of the substance of fetish value (see Figure 5.1). Abstract labor is not simply de-concretized or de-skilled labor but rather a derivative form of work devoid of content and creativity. It emerged in a communal context with minimal conviviality and solidarity and represents the exchange-value of labor power of laborers dispossessed of their autonomous agency to sustain their lives as part of the life-domain and to determine their own fate prefiguratively. In those production relations where the involved (reproductive) labor is not directly commodified as wage labor, even if no value-added is produced, the fetish value continues to grow as an augmented deficit caused by the demolition of the commoning basis of (more than) human creative work.

Labor Detained in the Mechanical Structure of Capital

As posited earlier, capital first reifies human creativity into labor power through the decommonization infra-process (i.e., primary abstraction and primary appropriation) and then into 'abstract labor' – which is contained in both material and immaterial commodities – through valorization and realization processes. For this to occur, capital must first enclose the material commoning sources of more-than-human liveability, displace convivial relationships, and politically subjugate the emerging classes of workers in order to weaken their prefigurative power for alterity. This is because all four causal elements of labor are rooted in the four commoning sources of true value (see Figure 5.2). Materially, labor cannot exist without relying on the liveable sources of the life-domain. For labor to become decommonized, these sources must also be decommonized. The early historical manifestation of this process in the case of England (the "usurpation of common lands," "expropriation of agricultural populations from the land," and creation of "rightless laborers" and a "home market for industrial capital") was explicitly discussed by Marx in the final part of *Capital, Volume 1*.

Depriving the agents of the creative power of their natural integration with the sources of liveability makes them dependent on capital for their survival and biosocial reproduction. It is, therefore, essential for capital to enclose the material causes of liveability, not just to extract their natural

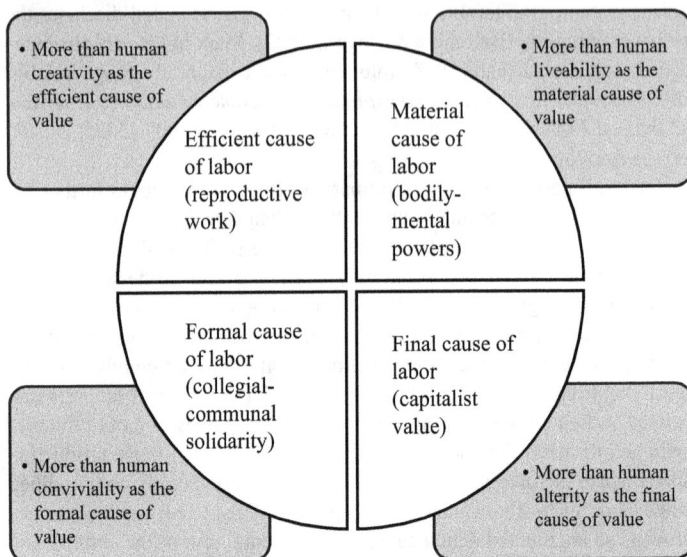

Figure 5.2 The causal structure of labor as decommonized creative power and its rootedness in the four commoning causes of true value.

riches but also to make the primary abstraction and appropriation of creative power possible. Sources of liveability alongside the convivial sources of life-making are then peripheralized as the so-called 'conditions of possibility' for the reproduction of labor. According to Marx, this should always chronologically precede "capitalist accumulation; an accumulation which is not the result of the capitalist mode of production but its point of departure" (Marx, 1990, p. 873).

David Harvey (2004) famously theorized the reinvention of this process in all possible new forms, such as neoliberal structural adjustments and austerity regimes, under the title of "accumulation by dispossession." Capital has been inherently dependent on dispossessing commons (as 'common resources') for constant accumulation (Harvey, 2003). From the commonist framework point of view, 'dispossession,' like the enclosure of the common lands and natural commons, only partly represents the appropriation process (as defined in the previous chapter). Marx and Harvey concentrate on the objective manifestation of a much deeper process which we may call 'accumulation by decommonization'. Labor, natural resources as commodities such as land, reproductive work from household to the public sector to the market relations, and the political organization of modern society from corporatized workplaces to international politics are the reified-fetishized products of the decommonizing infra-processes of the four causes of true value. They are respectively located in the manipulative, exploitative, extractivist, and domineering (MEED) power structures of capital (cf. Figure 4.3). Their production happens outside the 'capitalist mode of production,' as Marx claims, through what we may call the 'capitalist mode of decommonization.' Capital is inherently dependent on decommonization, that is the perversion of the commoning nature of the fundamental sources of value. And, as argued previously, all four arenas of decommonization are essentially interdependent (Figure 4.3); one cannot happen without the others also happening, and conversely, one cannot be reversed/liberated without the others also being reversed/liberated.

According to Marx, being disconnected from the rest of nature and incorporated into the mazes of capital laborers' communal senses of interconnectedness are replaced with capitalist social relations mediated by their products (material or immaterial) and the social forms of fetish value like money/wage. The incorporation of *oikos* into capitalist relations reifies it into what is known as the economy. This process is more than just a discursive construction in bourgeois economics, and therefore, cannot be negated by merely changing our economic thoughts. Under capitalism, the commoning causes of conviviality and creativity lose their organic connections with one another. The dislocation of working people from their natural communities and habitats (*oikoses*) significantly weakens their conviviality, i.e., their ability to live in communal solidarity with each other and non-human beings while negotiating their differences.

Capital encloses and reifies the commoning sources of conviviality to generate fetish value. The process is incomplete without the abstraction and appropriation of the commoning sources of alterity, i.e., the potentialities for prefigurative imagination and autonomous future-oriented decision-making, morally conscientious of the needs and rights of the (transcendental and imminent) Other, i.e., all living and even non-living beings, inclusive of future generations. The so-called productive laborers give up their willpower and real autonomy and hand over their imaginative power to capital, which politically disincentivizes them.

> Dreams of individual accomplishment and desires to contribute to the common good become firmly attached to waged work, where they can be hijacked to rather different ends ... the wage relation generates not just income and capital, but disciplined individuals, governable subjects, worthy citizens, and responsible family members.
>
> (Weeks, 2011, p. 8)

While the politics of labor and class struggles remain relevant, they primarily revolve around distributive conflicts concerning the allocation of labor's share within the capitalist value produced.

Capital, in Nancy Fraser's terms (2022), "devours" not only the commodified labor (through "exploitation") but also the uncommodifiable, unquantifiable, and socialized sources of value such as the planet, care, public infrastructure, social and digital commons, democratic institutions, communal activities, and the peripheralized other (through "expropriation"). As Fraser argues, expropriation is not limited to the historical primitive accumulation by enclosure in the early stage of the rise of capitalism in Europe. Rather, it is an ongoing development (a hidden abode behind Marx's 'hidden abode'[12]) that makes the exploitation of labor possible. The double hidden abode functions as the "background conditions of possibility" for capital's inner organization (Fraser, 2014, p. 57). The contemporary global expansion of 'resource frontiers,' and 'sacrifice zones' in both global North and South exemplify this. New literature analyzing forms of 'global extractivism' is rapidly emerging to address this global process, entailing an ecocide–genocide nexus (Chagnon et al., 2022).

The four elements of the so-called productive capital's inner exploitative structure, according to Marx and listed by Fraser (2022), consist of so-called free labor (an efficient cause only in its concrete form), private ownership of the means of production (as the material cause), market (as the formal cause), and capital's inherent imperative for self-expansion (as the final cause). However, the entire exploitative structure of capital should be seen as an infra-process through which (more than) human creative power is reduced only to a bearer of capital's final cause behind the production of fetish value, alongside the decommonization of the other three fundamental spheres of organized life (as described in the previous chapters). This perspective helps us explore a much more delicate and deeper working of *capitality*.

One can concur with Fraser that 'expropriation' (confiscating others' assets, human and non-human) is an essential enabling condition for 'exploitation' (in the form of surplus labor) by underlying it and making it more profitable. Marx was acutely aware of this relationship and did not overlook its significance. It is also critical to emphasize that the 'exploitation' of labor and the entire political–economic system that relies on it also creates the conditions of the possibility for the 'expropriation' of the (more-than-human) subalterns, resulting in a two-way relationship. *At the core of this dialectical interplay between exploitation and expropriation lies the process of decommonization.* Marxist feminists and social reproduction theorists have long been making efforts to highlight the fact that issues like domestic violence and the double exploitation of life-making workers, waged and unwaged, are made possible in more sophisticated ways than ever in the context of the commodification and exploitation of laborers, many of whom are females (Mies, 1986).

Austerity regimes in the global North and structural adjustment programs in the global South have contributed to the underfunding of social reproductive services, including the protection of victims of domestic and racial violence, the privatization of public assets, and the corporatization of the public sector. These have resulted in less affordable living expenses, higher household debts (which feed back into capital), the semi-proletarianization of households, and the disappearance of the subsistence economy, causing mass dislocation of local natives, small self-sustaining, organic, and regenerative food production system, and more (Bhattacharya, 2017). All this has become possible in the context where the perversion of the commoning sources of creativity fuels the relentless expansion of capital.

Capital incorporates alienated labor (alienated from the moral fabric of living in commons) into its expropriation projects. Laborers, especially in the global core and the core islands of the global periphery, are beneficiaries of such mass looting, as social reproduction becomes more affordable for them, despite their stagnated wages and unstoppable household debt burden, thanks to the expropriation processes. The closer they are to the cores of the global North and South, the more they benefit. A significant portion of their wages is reinvested in the consumerist economy and finance capital markets, perpetuating and sustaining the processes of expropriation. The simple adoption of ethical consumption and boycotts, if they grow big enough and for a long period, may have some civilizing impacts on the capitalist expropriation process, but ironically, may contribute to the increase in the costs of living, which is why they usually lose steam quickly.

The reification and appropriation of (more than) human creative power in capitalist production relations helps capital to reify sources of more-than-human liveability since labor's alienation from nature strips nature of its powerful, conscientious agency against capital. The alienation of labor turns it into capital's proxy, making labor a condition of possibility for the direct extraction of value from sources of liveability, conviviality, and alterity. Here, the annexation of one indispensable source of value relative to the one subjected to direct capitalist value extraction is critical, and this constitutes *the colonialist feature of capital.*

However, 'late capitalism' has found systematic ways to become less dependent on commodified labor through new modes of fetish value production, by relatively or fully externalizing productive labor into the artificially manufactured realms of the so-called 'nature,' politics, and community; these peripheral or semi-peripheral realms supply the so-called free gifts necessary for the sustenance of capital. Capital has always had an innate tendency to prefer an uncommodified-yet-reified form of labor that can be brought under colonialist control over fully commodified labor since it does not have to pay for it. We may call this the self-purification of capital through which alienated labor, like alienated nature (to the extent possible), is thrown out of the inner organization of capital. Direct exploitation of labor is progressively being replaced with its annexation and colonization wherever possible. The labor that is excluded from being exploited directly through the secondary abstraction process within the inner organization of productive capital remains primarily abstracted and thereby continues to be the source of fetish value, as with nature and affective work.

The labor that remains commodified due to the lack of technological capacity or its unautomatable nature must be exhausted to the maximum possible level and deprived of physical and mental security to be kept submissive. *After all, the portion of wage labor (surplus labor) that is the source of surplus capitalist value is unpaid and thus an uncommodified (yet reified and appropriated) portion of labor power.* The commodification and exploitation of labor power is the condition of possibility for the appropriation of its unwaged portion. This portion is treated like a gift from human nature and is not essentially different from unwaged reproductive labor, except that it is directly recruited in commodity production relations. *Automation relocates labor power from exploitative commodity production relations to the peripheral realm of capital's colonial relations.*

However, the relationship between exploitation and expropriation is more than a functional one in which one side mechanistically assists the other side. The existential engagement of 'exploitation' and 'expropriation' is rooted in a deeper commensuration infra-process. The only reason this complementary relationship is possible is that it is rooted in a deeper infra-process of decommonization out of which (using Fraser's taxonomy) labor, and (the subaltern) nature, care, and modern politics are born as the abstracted and controlled forms of the sources of creativity, liveability, conviviality, and alterity, respectively. *The true liberation of each one of these four elements is dependent on the liberation of the rest 'only' through reinstating their (partly original, partly futuristic) commonist state of being.*

Sectors of the economy that remain outside of the direct influence of capital's inner exploitative apparatus, such as the public sector and even the big not-for-profit organizations, are progressively decommonized through corporatization from within. Despite being publicly owned and not being determined by exchange-value, laborers in these sectors, including civil servants in various fields such as healthcare, education, and academia, are often required to work well above the level necessary for their social reproduction. This is due to the execution of corporate plans, rather than cooperative ones, set by a powerful and ruthless managerial class with algorithm-powered management systems. These managers are often contracted on salaries comparable to those of corporate and finance sector CEOs.

The predatory managerial classes in these sectors mainly consist of individuals who have either transitioned from the corporate sector or perceive their positions as stepping stones to attain high-level executive roles in corporations. Their task is to maximize revenue through the maximum corporatization of these institutions. A significant portion of the extracted surplus is subsequently transferred to rentier and finance capital holders in exchange for various resources and services, including energy, finance/credit, land, equipment, digital platforms, construction, maintenance, security, consulting, business partnerships, and funding for joint community/industry projects. This is done in the ultimate interest of the corporate sector through contracts and subcontracts.

The managerial class in the public sector functions as a proxy of finance and rentier capital in the colonization of the public sector's reproductive relations, as well as in the indirect exploitation of their workers. Here, the role that the public sector plays as another subaltern sphere is *more than the provision of the background conditions* for the exploitation of labor in the private sector. The sector is decommonized, so the fetish value is extracted in parallel and even in greater amounts relative to the direct extraction of value from productive labor. However, none of this is possible without decommonizing the productive/creative power of the value producers and their organizational settings in such sectors. Due to the loss of the commoning type of horizontal and participatory governance – which defines value and determines the purpose as the final cause – capital, without being directly involved in non-capitalized and under-commodified realms of laboring, continues to profit. In this way, capital can achieve a higher rate of growth in money form than when it had to invest directly in variable capital (employment of labor power), and thus, would constantly be involved in class struggles.

The contradiction here is that the more the labor is under-waged, underemployed, deskilled, casualized, over-worked, and/or precariatized under corporate settings, the more the capacity of society to take part in the circulation of capital diminishes. It has thus become more imperative for capital to colonize the subaltern lifeworlds to extract value. As these lifeworlds become scarcer, capital moves toward discovering and decommonizing less tangible/visible commons (like the future in the case of reifying risk into speculative investments) and manufacturing artificial or pseudo-commons (like social media platforms or crypto assets) for the extraction of more value. The more the communal bonds and convivial sources of true value-making are dismantled (decommonized), the more the individuals are atomized, and thus the more they seek conviviality through the monopolized artificial/virtual spaces of social liaison. The rising urge for conviviality, originally suppressed by capital in real life by alienating individuals from their commoning sources of true value, is now a new opportunity for capital. The urge is an emergent demand to be met with the supply of virtual spaces for the creation of 'artificial commons' by online prosumers who contribute to the life of commons through their communicative actions.

The high-tech private digital platforms function like feudal serfdoms, in which the digital serfs become increasingly involved in the production of commodity information in exchange for being allowed to socialize on these virtual lands and to satisfy their needs for convivial relationships and communication. A better analogy can be drawn with colonization. The data produced through these relationships are seen as sources of raw materials by high-tech capital. Individuals are dispossessed of the data they generate (Thatcher et al., 2016). The product is produced through pseudo-commoning relationships. The private exchange of products derived from digital serfdoms does not determine or abstract the labor of the digital serfs. However, this does not imply that capitalism has regressed into a form of modern serfdom or feudalism, as the dominance of capital continues to perpetuate feudalistic relationships alongside patriarchal and racial ones. Throughout history, capitalism has exhibited feudalistic characteristics, which have become more prevalent and apparent to residents of the global North following a brief period of working-class embourgeoisement.

More particularly in the so-called developed world, substantial sections of population have become increasingly dependent on virtual space property under the ownership and control of high-tech capital to run their businesses and organize their financial life. They form a new class of workers who, instead of selling their labor power, sell the products of their labor. The boundaries between the value makers and value takers become more and more obscure, and "doubly free labor" is less and less applicable to the workers. A large portion of their revenue is taken by the rentier and finance capital associated with 'platform' capitalism. Class solidarity and class consciousness can hardly be found among this group of workers. Instead, by absorbing and being absorbed into capital as a mode of being (capitality), they are potentially the most suitable prey for the power-hungry right-wing populist elite (Hosseini et al., 2022).

Notes

1 This chapter reproduces the preprint paper titled *Labor Redefined* by Hosseini (2022b).
2 The use of 'work' here should not be confused with (waged) 'work' used in the postwork or antiwork literature, with negative connotation (Weeks, 2011).
3 As noted by De Angelis (2022).
4 The idea has already been praised by the *Economist*, embraced by the World Bank in producing its research outputs and incorporated into the real state discourse (Federici, 2019, p. 85).
5 Unfortunately, the voices with an upper hand in the commons movements, especially in the global North, seem to favor such a direction.
6 Marx, influenced by Darwin, viewed living beings' organs as their technological tools and introduced the concept of 'tools as organs' in reference to human beings. He believed that these tools were as essential to human metabolism as their organs, but only when they were under the direct control and stewardship of free human consciousness.
7 In a society where the 'value practices' of capital determine the final cause of value production and are supported by the social norms that fetishize economic growth, the 'value practices' of (remaining or regained) commons lose their capacities as the antithetical to capital.
8 The fact that international institutions like the World Bank acknowledge the importance of community-based management of the commons as a way of civilizing the relentless dominance of markets is arguably telling enough.
9 Normative subjectivity, more exclusively attributable to humans, is their capacity to effect change, through constant reflexive evaluation of their living conditions and of the future that the evolving trends of change point to. However, human beings cannot be seen as the only efficient cause of value since subjectivity (that is the

capacity for effecting change) is attributable to other non-human living beings. The life-domain is a mesh of interacting subjectivities.

10 Hyper-reality from our point of view is a distorted version of reality (not merely a mythological or forged symbolic or discursive/ideational presentation of reality) practiced among social actors, that functions to socially reproduce a dominant hierarchical power structure.

11 Marx already made a one-off theoretical attempt that can be readily applied to contemporary cases, as long as they resemble the production relations presupposed by him.

12 Marx's hidden abode is the wage-based production site where exploitation happens, behind the apparently free market–based exchange site (Marx, 1990, p. 279).

6 Recharting the Debates on Labor Theory of Value in Light of Smart Machines, Affect, and Climate Change

In this chapter, divided into three distinct sections, we investigate how the commonist approach contributes to the ongoing debates surrounding the relevance of the Marxian Labor Theory of Value (LTV) in the context of rising smart machines, the increasing importance of affect, and the growing ecological challenges faced by human civilization. Since the mid-twentieth century, the LTV has been questioned by critical theorists on two fronts. One has focused on the changing nature of capital post-Marx,[1] while the other has questioned the theory's incapacity to recognize sources of value other than wage labor, such as social and ecological reproduction. While there are overlaps between the two, the remedies either point to abandoning or limiting the use of the theory due to its fallacies or narrowness or to reinterpret it to make it applicable to all true sources of value and new features of capital. What we call the 'rejectionists' neither recognize any utility in the concept of value nor see wage labor as the ultimate source of value. The revisionists, meanwhile, draw on various reinterpretations of the theory, above all (various versions of) the so-called New Interpretation, to argue that the theory is still quantitatively applicable if correctly interpreted and/or that the disparate seeds of its qualitative reconstruction are detectable across Marx's works.

It is beyond the scope of this book to engage deeply in those debates or present a detailed review of them. We will, however, briefly discuss the major lines of dispute and the implications of the commonist perception of value for overcoming them, arguing that the commonist modular framework can help us avoid some of the underlying confusion.

The Labor Theory of Value in the Age of Smart Machines: Reinterpretation, Abandonment, or Reconstruction?

Marx begins *Capital* with the commodity as a modern form of objectified human labor in capitalism. It can be analyzed in terms of its dual nature, being the source of use-value and value at the same time, the latter being necessarily represented as exchange-value. This duality of value is rooted in the bifurcation of labor into concrete labor and abstract labor. Abstract labor, expressed as the socially necessary labor time to produce commodities, is the common

DOI: 10.4324/9781003340386-6

denominator embedded in exchanged commodities, making them commensurable despite their qualitative differences. Workers sell their labor power (capacity to work) as a commodity, and therefore, their labor power is valued in terms of the labor time necessary for its reproduction. However, unlike other commodities, labor power can produce value. Any quantity of value created beyond the average labor time socially necessary for the reproduction of labor is surplus value. Surplus value is the origin of aggregate profit appropriated and accumulated by the capitalist class.

Capital constantly strives to maximize profit by extending the working hours or by intensifying the laboring process through automation/mechanization, which results in shortening the labor time necessary for the reproduction of labor. Thus, under capitalism, ownership, and control over the means of production, rather than political dominance, becomes the 'primary' source of power. The formation of a 'social class' of people who must sell their labor power in exchange for wages becomes possible. The 'working class' is existentially dependent on the means of production while at the same time being excluded from controlling it. The power of capital lies in its ability to control the working class by alienating them from their capacity to work and from the products of their work. However, the exploitation of workers is not the only aspect of what Marx's value theory tries to grasp, as Harvey (2018a) argues, the theory "focuses on the consequences of value operating as a regulatory norm in the market for the experience of labourers condemned by their situation to work for capital."

The standard interpretation of Marx's LTV views the substance of value as the labor time contained in commodities. Accordingly, no capitalist value is produced if no labor time is directly contained in privately owned commodities with social use-value, made through privately owned and controlled social production for the mere purpose of private exchange. The demise of the role of living labor in the generation of capital in late capitalist modes of production poses a serious challenge to the LTV, making it inadequate or redundant (according to some critics), if not totally refuting it (according to other critics). The conditions that pose such a challenge are those in which: labor loses ground to the machine in an increasingly automated and smart mode of capitalist production; the division of labor is decentralized; work is socialized, and the boundaries between production and reproduction are obscured; work is precaritized; the prominence of material products is overtaken by the immaterial ones showing a strong tendency to reduce the share of wage labor to almost zero since they can be reproduced indefinitely by a negligible amount of labor; and finally, rent and interest, bypassing commodity production, have become the dominant bases of revenue and capital growth.

Post-Marxists (post-structuralist and critical theorists) as well as autonomist Marxists have been among the more radical critics of LTV arguing for its abandonment. The crux of their criticisms is their emphasis on the role of advanced technologies in transforming the capitalist mode of production beyond dependence on productive labor. Capital is now significantly more capable of extracting value out of the so-called unproductive socio-ecological sphere.[2] "Machines and algorithms manage the value chain and concrete human labour is less and less necessary – allegedly" (Wimmer, 2020, p. 287). Some argue that this new format of capitalism makes prior labor theories of value obsolete. Negri and Hardt (2004, p. 150) argue that "[i]n the paradigm of immaterial production, the theory of value cannot be considered in terms of measured quantities of time, so exploitation cannot be understood in these terms." Marx's LTV becomes superseded, according to Negri (1988) since both production and reproduction have been subsumed into capital. As productive labor gives way to 'socialized work,' the whole process of social reproduction (social life) becomes subject to commodification. As this intensifies, the labor of social reproduction turns increasingly into a type of abstract labor that can no longer be assessed under the capitalist factory regime of time. As the measurement of value becomes random in the absence of any objective criterion, such as labor time, control over the workers' labor power returns to its political form (Negri & Emery, 2018, p. 18). In the case of social media, for example, those who follow this argumentation, like Arvidsson and Colleoni (2012), do not see the affective work and financial speculations of the users as dependent on their labor time. According to them, such work only adds value to the brand of companies, and thus Marx's LTV is deemed irrelevant.[3]

Against such a radical departure from LTV, and to overcome its limitations in dealing with sources of value other than direct/living wage labor, revisionists have proposed (1) expanding the notion of labor to be inclusive of "any alienated, coerced and boundless work [that] amounts to an expenditure of abstract labour and thus creates value for capital" (De Angelis, 1995; Kay, 2007);[4] or (2) analytically differentiating between what 'adds value,' that is living/direct labor, and what 'has value,' that is, indirect/past labor (embedded in non-labor inputs). The 'New Interpretation'[5] argues that non-labor inputs like the rest of nature, technology, applied science, and affective work only transfer their value – as embedded indirect/past labor – to the end product through labor. But, "there cannot be value-added if there is no direct (living) labour" (Rotta & Paraná, 2022, p. 1047).[6] Moreover, Marx was concerned with the long-term scope and macro scale of capital. "Marx's *Capital* shows that surplus value can be produced in one industry yet realized as profit (and possibly revenue) by other industries over the course of circulation" (Cogliano, 2018, p. 505). Therefore, the fact that some sectors of the economy undergo substantial automation or digitalization does not mean that labor is wiped out of the whole picture, nor that its role is meaningfully minimized.

In the case of corporate social media, those inspired by the New Interpretation school (Rigi & Prey, 2015) argue that no value is 'added' through the involvement of the prosumers with the corporate social media platforms. Value, they argue, is transferred only from one commodity form to another. However, the revenue made in such virtual spaces and the value-added of 'brands' can still be understood in terms of the roles of monopoly rentier capitalism, extra profit, and fictitious capital. This view rejects the idea that the users/'prosumers' of social media produce value and surplus value by spending their labor time, creating data, and/or turning themselves into "audience commodities," whose surplus time spent on watching ads generates surplus value (as advocated by Fuchs, 2010; Fuchs & Mosco, 2016). They warn against conflating the general surplus value produced at the point of production with its particular manifestation in the realm of distribution.[7]

According to those who draw on the New Interpretation, Marx differentiated between value and price, and therefore, the growth in the income or profit of companies that produce immaterial commodities (such as digital information (DI), almost fully automated with almost zero labor time involved) cannot be interpreted as an increase in the extraction of surplus value and rate of exploitation. The fully automated infinite replication of immaterial commodities cannot be fully explained by the Marxian value theory.[8] The production of immaterial commodities only transfers value from pools of surplus value that are already created in other sectors. For instance, cryptocurrencies should be seen as digital assets, rather than money, that have value but no value-added since their production and speculation "draw from the existing global pool of value-added" (Rotta & Paraná, 2022, p. 1046). This is because the process does not directly derive from production relations and requires no direct living labor. However, as assets, they do contain capitalist value. The origin of this value lies in the electricity (the labor of nature) expended in their mining, the surplus value of surplus labor solidified in the energy production process in the required computational equipment and warehousing, as well as the social reproductive labor that underpins all the above sources. With the increase in the costs of mining cryptocurrencies, they have shifted to places where electricity is heavily subsidized by the state (i.e., the global South), resulting in the extraction of massive quantities of value out of nature and public resources for funding social-ecological reproduction. Therefore, the decommonization of the sources of conviviality and liveability and their perversion into the sources of fetish value has accelerated.

Those who argue for abandoning LTV base their arguments on perceiving the new advancements in capitalism as transmutations in the nature of capital. However, the history of capitalism reveals that automation, driven by competition and capital's inherent urge for maximizing profit, has been a constant feature of capitalism. As Benanav (2020, p. 7) reminds us, "the same is not true of the theory of a coming age of automation, which extrapolates from instances of technological change to a broader account of social transformation." Failing to adequately grasp the nature of capital results in a linear episodic perception of the history of capital.

But what are the implications of the commonist framework for comprehending the complexities of capital that pose challenges to LTV? Many

Marxist theorists concentrate on the quantitative aspect of Marx's theorization of mechanization, which is the translation of the alteration in the value and technical composition of capital into a general fall of the rate of profit and the contradictory consequences for both capital and labor. The qualitative aspects of the phenomenon that can be extracted from Marx's method are less well-received. Marx did not see automation as simply causing unemployment. Rather, he noted its 'potential' impact in the form of the displacement of labor from more capital-intensive to more labor-intensive industries that we identify today as the service sector, which is arguably more involved in value circulation than value production. However, even the mass relocation of laborers may be caused by political–economic factors other than automation (see the study by Benanav, 2020).[9]

Machines, as 'dead labor' are made and maintained by living labor. They are thus ossified surplus values extracted from the labor involved in the creation of their use-value. However, at the micro level of automatized firms/sectors, the more dead labor is employed, the more the share of surplus value (extracted out of the living labor) in increased productivity and profit declines. If labor is perceived as the only source of value in the automated sector, the LTV will fail to explain the growth of capital in the context of the decline in the share of labor unless we expand the scope to the aggregate/macro level. However, as explained later in this chapter, we may argue that greater 'fetish value' is produced in money form, as capital becomes more independent from living labor by converting it into an externality to be absorbed/compensated by not only the more labor-intensive sectors of the economy but also by the community, civil society institutions, political organizations through civilizing mechanisms, and the rest of nature.

More fundamentally, we may contend that automation or mechanization, for Marx, was a mechanism for extending control over the labor process through the objectification of the division of labor. The automatized factory, according to Marx, was a "prime mover capable of exerting any amount of force while retaining perfect control" (Marx, 1990, p. 506; cited in Smith, 2022, p. 137). Automation is a radical reformatting that usually deskills the laborer, reducing them to operators and depriving them of their specialized subjective labor power, knowledge, and associated potentialities for resistance. But even when deskilling is not significant, the more that work is automated, the less autonomy workers exercise. This means that the 'primary abstraction' of human creative power is further infiltrated into the commodity production relations, through which labor loses its organized prefigurative power and convivial base to determine the final cause of production, that formerly was manifested in their unionism, tempering capital's final cause – endless growth – with their own welfare.

The subjectivity of human creative power and its skillful mastery over the means of production (to the extent they are free from any means of control) is rooted in the commonality of living in convivial relations. The idea of machines evolving from tools to workers, creating a 'post-work' future, is a hyperbole (Wajcman, 2022). But machines gaining greater functionality as means of subjugation (mostly through the precarization of occupations and decentralization of production lines resulting in less workplace conviviality) has always been the case in capitalist modes of production. This constitutes another pathway for the infiltration of primary abstraction into production relations.

The deeper reification of labor made possible by post-human technology (techno-colonialist capital) reduces the share of the secondarily abstracted labor in the extraction of capitalist value from the mechanized production process. However, this also increases the 'primary abstraction' of excluded labor through new modes of re-engaging peripheralized labor. This reification of human creative power is complemented by fetishization, in which dead labor (machines) appears as a source of value worthy of 'investment,' while living labor is perceived as a cost. Therefore, the efficient causality of labor and the formal causality of workplace solidarity (as the remaining elements of the commoning nature of collective work) are further reduced to material causality, making workers more easily interchangeable with one another and with machines. The issue of alienation becomes even more prominent here. Automation, when manifested under the command of high tech, is a dehumanizing process that significantly compromises (more than) human capacities for creative, moral, and aesthetic reasoning over a long healthy life and achieving such a life (in balance with the embedded self, the other, community, and the rest of nature) (Al-Amoudi, 2022; Demichelis & Caution, 2022).

Increased automation at the micro level of productive/industrial firms results in the reduction of the value of productive/industrial labor power as variable capital. As this becomes a new norm across the entire advanced capitalist economy, the way will be paved for greater exploitation of labor and the extraction of surplus value under more precarious conditions in more labor-intensive sectors. This issue paradoxically discourages investment in technological innovation in sectors with cheapened labor and nature.

As some types of machines or automation systems become popular, a new generation of ancillary industries grows to produce, train, and educate them, supply energy and parts, and provide services that are not productive (e.g., circulation and supervision). They would add to the demand for labor. However, these industries often rely on outsourcing their needs to and from developing societies (i.e., the global South), which offer cheaper labor (often due to lax regulations) and abundant natural resources (often with weak environmental laws). Wherever outsourcing is not possible, these services are left to be provided by the public, small business, and not-for-profit sectors with thin profit margins, per the inflamed costs of operation and dictated by monopoly rentier and finance capital. These activities, contrary to what Marx assumed (Smith, 2022, pp. 148–149), are not major costs to capital but rather to society, i.e., socialized costs that contribute to the private accumulation of capital.

The stagnation of real wages in the developed world despite significant increases in automation-induced productivity over the past few decades is common knowledge. With the import of cheapened resources and manufactured goods from the recently industrialized global South, the surplus abstract labor/value is imported, making the costs of living more bearable for the working class in the North, which is another civilizing mechanism that increases stability in the context of increasing public economic austerity. Capital treats redundant labor as a social externality for which it refuses to bear responsibility and costs.[10] Any social externalities dealt with by any party except capital become an uncompensated source of fetish value for capital, similar to the contribution of the rest of nature and life-making labor to the reproduction of commodified labor. In industries where automation of the production process and deskilling are impossible or overly costly, automation is used as a managerial tool to exercise higher control over staff through commanding, monitoring, and ranking workers as staff performance. As a result, despite remaining skillful, the laborer is further pressured to become a mere cog in the managerial machinery.

The subordination of laborers to the will of capital through mechanization also distorts their ability to decide on the purpose of their collective work in tune with their broader communal purposes and thus deprives them of their ability to determine and realize the final cause of living well in common. The division of labor, or the organization of work as the formal cause of value production, is reshaped through automation. In other words, capital constantly remakes the production process in its own image (Smith, 2022, p. 140). More importantly, automation accelerates the infiltration of capital's final cause into the entire causal structure of labor in the commodity production process. *The automation process across the economy should be seen as turbocharging the decommonization of (more-than) human creative power and thus decomposing the potentialities to produce true value.*

Time determines work (Mella Méndez & Carby-Hall, 2020). Capital plays a decisive teleological causal role by changing the temporal structure of work, thereby imposing its logic (growth for the sake of growth) on the production relations to secure the making of capitalist value. This is now much more pronounced in the so-called gig economy. Concerning the work of the rest of nature, capital desynchronizes chronobiological rhythms, resulting in the loss of life's 'natural' control/agency over and through time. Time is no longer tuned with the natural rhythms of ecological and social reproduction.

Automation is also linked to the intensification and acceleration of value extraction from the sources of liveability, including the material causality of labor (from its bio-physiological concreteness to the affective work of workers' households and community) and the material causality of the rest of nature (and the metabolic harmony between human labor and nature). The relocation of wage labor from being an insider of direct exploitative production relations to an outsider, through changes in the composition of capital (peripheralization/annexation of labor), *increases primary abstraction relative to secondary abstraction.* While a decline in secondary abstraction may lead to a reduction in the rate or mass of surplus value (and thus the rate of profit) extracted from labor at the macro level, it simultaneously enhances the share of other decommonized sources of value in the reproduction of capital. Consequently, the rate and mass of fetish value continue to rise, perpetuating a state of supremacy within the system.

Machines may increase labor productivity (output per worker) and thus decrease the surplus capitalist value extracted from living direct labor. But this is outweighed by the increase in ecological and reproductive surplus value. And we have not yet taken the future as another source of value into account. As automation over-accelerates the perversion of true value into capitalist value at a speed far greater than the pace of the life-domain for its own healthy regeneration (under the commonist state of living), future risks accumulate at an exponential rate. This leads to a greater loss of the commoning capacities of the life-domain for producing true value; a colossal deficit that must be incorporated into our value theory. Part of this risk is commodified in the form of insurance commodities, commercialized ecological offsets and credits, bonds, and derivatives, enabling the prefigurative behaviors of those involved in these markets to become the bearers of capitalist value (Christophers, 2016). Here, the future as a commons of alterity is primarily abstracted and appropriated.

The primary abstraction of human creativity is always at work as part of the infra-process of decommonization. Thus, even uncommodified forms of human productivity such as the self-employed labor of digital platform drivers in the gig economy, data-producing activities of social media prosumers under platform/cloud capital, or the algorithmically managed work of a university educator become (primarily) abstracted and thus perverted into reified generators of fetish value. Critics like Yanis Varoufakis and others have been quick to consider this type of labor as one of the key signs of rising 'modern serfdom' under what is considered to be neo- or 'techno-feudalism' replacing capitalism (Wark, 2019; Dean, 2020; Varoufakis, 2021).[11] This 'endism' rests upon an idealistic perception of capitalism as a system based on free and fair competition overtaken by monopolies, assisted by the state. However, from a commonist point of view, the fundamental features or nature of capital have not changed. New technological advancements only give new manifestations to these fundamental features or change the architecture of capital but not its essence.

The period in Western capitalist history during which capital became, albeit temporarily, more competitive and less oligopolistic marked a brief ascendancy of its progressive civilizing forces. This occurred after the Great Depression and two devastating World Wars fought among imperialist (regressive civilizing) powers. *For most of its history, however, capital has been, and increasingly will be, dependent on the feudalistic/colonialist relationship with the un-commodified/un-commodifiable work of human and non-human beings.* This is because primary abstraction and appropriation are central to capital. The infiltration of primary abstraction into the inner organization of commodity production relations by replacing the secondary abstraction of labor (through precariatization and automation of work) in the global core zones coexists with the expansion and escalation of secondary abstraction of labor in labor-intensive, low-labor-cost industries of the global periphery.

The precarious freelance labor power in the gig economy may no longer be bought by capital as a commodity through direct stable employment in the production process. However, it is still abstracted via meta-mechanisms other than the private production-exchange nexus. The laborer is given some degree of autonomy and self-rule as a so-called freelancer. They market directly to sell the product of their creative work that embodies their labor power. Their creative work, reified but not commodified, is primarily abstracted and appropriated, rather than secondarily. They are turned into a pawn for capital, which requires them to internalize the logic of capital (capitality). Work is socialized for them, but the final cause of capital is internalized through self-exploitation and the exploitative treatment of those below them.

Big business capital provides the 'economically-dependent-executively-autonomous' workers with a platform for petty profit-seeking activities. This way, rentier capital gains ascendancy through seeking rent from labor instead of directly employing/buying its power (labor power) as a commodity. This process of decommonizing (through annexing de-/under- commodified) human creative power has gained greater momentum with the advancements of high-tech apparatuses, which serve as the already appropriated common infrastructures for the production of new fetish value.

The increase in the money supply by central banks has intensified in the post-GFC and more so in the post-COVID era(s). This intensification has also accelerated the growth of corporate monopolies and made their profit-seeking activities less dependent on the infra-process of perverting human creativity into productive labor. It has opened the gates for the expansion of rentier capital and the transformation of labor into a mode of work that has a strong resemblance to serfdom. The idealism of competitive markets is being increasingly shattered. But this is not new. Indeed, Marx putatively started from the key idealistic classical presumptions about 'capitalist freedom' to show the inevitability of the cruelty and contradiction that emerges from them when they are operationalized in reality. Capitalism has consistently fallen short of the ideals often attributed to it.

Social Reproduction Theory: A Commonist Reflection

The Social Reproduction Theory (SRT) can roughly be categorized into two main perspectives. One perspective, championed by Mariarosa Dalla Costa,

Silvia Federici, and Selma James, among others, argues that domestic labor generates value and, as such, must be compensated (see Fortunati & Fleming, 1995; Rodríguez-Rocha, 2021). According to this approach, the notions of capitalist value and value source should be expanded to the already estranged zones that are not directly subjected to private ownership, commodification, and/or the private exchange of commodities for profit-making. These are the zones of precariatized labor in the so-called non-productive sector, unwaged social reproduction labor from the household to the public and civil society sectors, common pools of material and immaterial riches from natural resources to datafied records of communal digital interactions, and political institutions and struggles that determine societal desires and define the 'good life.'

The other perspective, which is influenced by Lisa Vogel (1983) and is further developed by Tithi Bhattacharya (2017), argues that social reproduction constitutes a prerequisite for value production rather than being a direct source of capitalist value. This perspective aligns more closely with Marx's approach in *Volume 1* of *Capital*, and as a result, situates life-making activities outside the confines of capital's inner workings, acknowledging their potential for catalyzing a deeper transformation. For example, by employing the 'dual engagement' concept, this perspective recognizes that while care work can be commodified and integrated into capitalist production relations as care labor, it can also remain engaged in non-capitalist life-making activities and production of true value.

The division in SRT is rooted in the fact that both sides overlook the fact that in *Capital*, Marx 'intentionally' focuses on the inner organization of capital (exclusive of social reproduction relations) rather than capitalist social relations where the reproduction of the working class happens as a socio-historical specificity (see Gimenez, 2018). But neither of these two SRT veins differentiate between true value and fetish value. Both presume one single notion of value as constructed under capital's terms. Each implies different theories of change; considering domestic labor as a source of value would encourage demands for financial compensation while placing domestic labor outside the realm of capital would provoke the creation of autonomous care-centered economies. Interestingly, however, both contribute to the civilizing mechanisms of capital.

The former approach does so by demanding a share of the surplus value civilizing capital by making it responsive to sustaining the reproduction of labor power. However, at the same time, it helps reify domestic labor power and increases aggregate demand necessary for the growth of capital.[12] As Foster and Burkett warn (2018, p. 7), such an approach misses the "point of the specifically reified character of value in a capitalist society, the source of its increasingly distorted 'creative destruction' of the world at large."

The latter approach views domestic labor as a prerequisite for liberatory praxis, which remains dependent on capital to sustain it until wage labor is fully abolished. This places unwaged domestic labor, alongside the public sector and civil society, in the service of recycling capital's negative externalities by producing positive externalities (such as enhancing the communal quality of life, reproduction of labor power, knowledgeable minds, etc.) back into the system. Both perspectives see the abolition of wage labor as their ultimate goal, which is crucial for their transformative potential. However, their theories of change in this regard have little to do with their value theories.

The two approaches in SRT would be improved, from our perspective, if they expanded their ontological views beyond the mechanical structure of capital. Commodified labor is deeply entangled with reproductive social labor, and thus, the relationship is bilateral. According to Figure 4.3, *the perversion of human creative power into human labor through the socio-economic infra-process of decommonization is not possible unless the organic configuration of the commonist state of living is perverted into the mechanical structure of capitalist relations.* Only then can they function as socio-cultural conditions of possibility for the emergence of labor and the exploitation of labor power. It is then that social reproduction, an alienated form of decommonized conviviality, becomes a background condition of possibility for the production and exploitation of productive labor. However, this is not a one-way relationship. Dialectically, the infra-process of decommonizing convivial relations into social reproductive relations in the modern family or community finds wage labor and the associated economic production relations as its own socio-economic condition of possibility. The so-called productive labor is employed not just to produce surplus (fetish) value but also to function as a proxy of capital for the continuation of de-essentializing social and ecological reproduction.

It is not just 'affective labor' that makes 'wage labor' possible, but also 'wage labor' that makes 'affective labor' possible, in the forms emptied from their original convivial essence and brought into non-productive capitalist relations. This is the root cause of a much deeper crisis than the shortage of care in modern society. Surely, affective relations in the alienated *oikos* do not completely disappear, and therefore there are always potentialities for resistance and restoring their essence. However, *the restoration of conviviality will depend on restoring the commoning essence of the other three sources of value.*

Unwaged affective work is dependent on the household income (wage) and has little choice in the nuclear family structure but to spend that wage to draw on commodified materials and the energy extracted from the sources of liveability to meet its material and immaterial needs and desires. These needs and desires are socially constructed in accordance with the imperatives of living under capitalism and are cognitively reinforced by the capitalist machinery of imagineering prosperous futures. These mutual dependencies restructure household relations so that they become the bearers of the capitalist final cause. Likewise, other areas of social reproduction beyond household and community, such as public welfare and social security services, are existentially dependent on national and state revenues, themselves generated through the socio-economic decommonization of (more-than-human) creative power. Public infrastructures and services, which are structurally dependent on and subservient to capitalist economic growth, consume massive amounts of natural resources and significantly contribute to climate change and the degradation of ecosystems. During financial crises, public investment, supercharged by creating massive financial and ecological debts, takes on the role of a savior. The policies that underpin these social reproductive services are directed toward protecting capital. In this way, state-funded social reproduction becomes a civilizing mechanism, adding to the stability of the system and reducing the need for highly destabilizing overt state violence and nakedly coercive power. In Fraser's terms (2022), capital "cannibalizes" social, political, and ecological wealth in the zones behind/beyond the economy. But perhaps more critically, what underpins this cannibalization is that capital restructures these zones in its own image, emptying them of their commonist essence so that, together with alienated labor, they contribute to the making of fetish value. In other words, zones of social reproduction that exist outside of capitalist commodified relations and have commoning features are being *annexed* to the realm of capital. This can be referred to as capital's *annexation of non-commodified zones of commoning* in its socio-ecological frontiers, which is necessary for their constant decommonization, the hidden abode behind Fraser's hidden abode!

Post-structuralist feminists take the route of substantial disengagement with capital by focusing on the realms of un- or under-colonized spaces such as community economy and unpaid domestic work (Gibson-Graham, 1996; Gibson, et al., 2015), hoping that the creation of capital-free autonomous niches of communal life would amount to a full systemic change. The post-developmentalist pluriverse perspective follows the same logic. The nature–society, ecology–economy, and productive–reproductive dualisms are not just intellectual and discursive structures. They are also *strategies of power rooted in the structures of capital*. Therefore, achieving nondualism requires more than a change in our perceptions and discourses and even more than building exemplary moments and isolated spaces of practicing nondualism; *it requires strategizing against the power of capital*.

Any liberation of our imaginations from what we call 'fetish value' under capital may look like an improvement but will end up being a setback if achieved at the cost of profound disengagement with the political realities of capital and the struggles of the working class. As the post-class politics of politically disenchanted leftist movements grow, not only the productive forces but also unwaged reproductive laborers (traditional and precarious) in the global North, under Fordism or post-Fordism, and in the fast-industrializing global South, find no solid ideological base, no strong common system of values, no vernacular language that relates to their daily life experiences, and no unblemished ways of constructing functional alliances with middle-class post-modernists, post-developmentalists, post-Marxists, and even revivalist Marxists who have (sub)consciously inherited a value-free notion of value from *Capital*. Working classes, when deserted by the new left, now increasingly turn to their last resort among social democrats, who are rather marginalized in their own reformist political parties, and the nationalist–populists who have been gaining the upper hand by radicalizing conservative parties or establishing their own parties (Hosseini et al., 2022). The COVID-19 pandemic exposed not only the shortcomings of the system in safeguarding the lives of millions of people but also the continuing inadequacies of many counter-system movements in channeling the working class's distrust of the state, corporate sector, and the elite into a powerful, radically transformative political force resistant to the lure of radical populism (Gray & Gills, 2022).

Despite these reservations, the post-structural and neo-anarchist ethics and value systems provide us with a highly insightful and rich set of ideas that can underpin the normative aspects of the commonist approach to value theory. They can help us imagine, explore, and establish commonist ways of living where the four indispensable sources of true value are fully functional. Such an image is not historically rootless. Quite the contrary. The social anthropological, archaeological, and historical accounts of past and present struggles to produce true value have disclosed and will continue to unveil the presence of the functionalities and transformative potentialities of indispensable commons. Literary, aesthetic, theological, and philosophical examinations of societal dreams and reflections on the metaphysical implications of the outcomes of evolutionary biology, quantum physics, and cosmology should be employed in our efforts in this direction.

The results must also be coupled with critical analyses of how capital operates and evolves. While it is incorrect to define the harsh reality of capital solely as the absence or suppression of ideal alternatives, it is also problematic to exclude from our analysis of capital the truthful images that naturally arise from collective dreams, practices, values, norms, desires, needs, and struggles of historical counter-movements. The abstract concept of value provides a unique advantage in making this integration possible, as 'value' is where *the real* and *the ideal* intersect.

The negation of linear thinking about the historical development of social formations, the recognition of the (principles of) deep interconnectedness of the life-domain, the acknowledgment that every individual being is a being-in-common or a becoming-in-common, and nondualism form the basis of pluriversalist thinking. This is a new paradigm that should be embraced in the commonist value theory. However, when these principles are applied to the new paradigm itself, the result is more modesty and more integrity. Pluriversalism will find its own location in the broader commonist paradigm. Only then will it supply the values that can underpin our normative vision of what constitutes true value as opposed to fetish value and feed our alternative imaginations and help us understand the existing potentialities within the uncolonized territories of life.

The incorporation of the normative notion of value, which emerges out of alternative imaginaries, into our analyses of capital will show us a more comprehensive image of capital than that which the orthodox Marxist tradition portrays. Capital is more complex than the product and process of the extraction of surplus value out of living/direct labor. Rather, it is a fetish that functions as value, obscuring the true value of all the existing potentialities natural to humanity and the rest of nature for harmonious, inclusive, and sustainable self-fulfillment. Instead of defining capital by using the logic it imposes on life, we will be using the logic of life as a commons to reveal the true nature of capital.

All four fundamental sources of true value as commons naturally regenerate and sustain themselves. Under capital, these ultimate sources are qualitatively deprived of their self-regenerativity and quantitatively shortchanged; their capacity for meeting the basic requirements of their reproduction is compromised as a result of the over-extraction of capitalist value. This is no longer limited to commodified labor. It is true that wage labor 'adds value,' but value also needs other distinct types of causation to be fully realized. Value needs structure; it must have an objective/material embodiment or quality and has to play a function seen by society as a worthwhile end to pursue, by haunting the public's imagination. The ontological differences between these mechanisms of causing value should not be ignored; a flat-ontological perception of capitalist value that is highly problematic. The Aristotelian theory of causation helps us avoid falling into the reductionist flat ontology by ontologically differentiating between the four essential types of causation. In our theory, labor and class do not lose their defining role.

The Marxian notion of commodity value is based on the difference between the value required for the reproduction of labor in its decommonized forms and the total value extracted. However, the relationship between capital and the four fundamental sources of value is more complex than just the quantitative extraction and expropriation of commodity value. The difference between the value required for the regeneration of the fundamental sources of value after their perversion and the value extracted from their combination can be considered as 'surplus capitalist value,' which in this case is a much wider and multidimensional notion than the Marxian one. The four ultimate causes of value are interdependent in the production of true value. Under capitalism, their commoning essence transmutes into properties of capital, and their harmony with one another is compromised. Their capacity to exist and function as commons, producing true value as their fuel or blood, is damaged. Regeneration turns into degeneration. The return of any portion of capitalist value through civilizing mechanisms such as wages, environmental rehabilitation programs, and welfare spending to increase their endurance is deployed only to slow down their degeneration and ultimately sustain capitalism for a longer period.

Eco-centric Revisions and Revitalizations of Marxian Value Theory

Apart from the "first-stage ecosocialists" identified by Foster (2022), who call for rejecting Marx's value theory based on its perceived ecological blind spots, there are two contrasting approaches to revising the theory. This dichotomy bears a resemblance to the divergent perspectives within the SRT camp discussed earlier. The first approach advocates the integration of nature into Marxian value theory. Ecosocialists such as Jason W. Moore, eco-Sraffian value theorists, and the non-Marxian energy-value school in ecological economics are among the groups that support this view (Burkett, 2006, pp. 16–17).

The second perspective, however, rejects the idea of ascribing capitalist value to natural resources. This includes Marxist revivalists like Foster and Burkett, who see nature as one of the major objective conditions of the possibility for production, but also non-Marxist ecological economists influenced by Herman Daly. Among the former group, some, by following Marx's differentiation between use-value and exchange-value, recognize nature only as a source of 'use-value' and wealth.[13] What constitutes value under capital is the exchange-value or abstract labor. Ecological economists following Daly, on the other hand, do not consider any objective factor in production, including labor, as a source of value. They define value teleologically as the 'enjoyment of life,' which is the ultimate benefit of every economic activity.

The above-mentioned first approach of attributing value to nature is not without major limitations. When nature's value is defined through 'private exchange,' capitalist value is ascribed, which leads to the disregard of nature's intrinsic value or the conflation of the two types of value. In a capitalist system, nature is ultimately commodified and subjected to market valuation, ultimately being fetishized as 'ecological/natural capital.' The theory subsequently argues that, similar to labor, nature is exploited and depleted beyond its regenerative capacity. Nature is reduced to constant capital as reflected in Marx's famous equation of the rate of profit, and due to the inherent constant pursuit of profit, is overly cheapened and thus exploited (Moore, 2015; see Saito, 2017b: for his criticism of Moore's ecological value theory). The result is additional surplus value. The theory, as Foster and Burkett (2018) argue, suffers from an ontologically monistic treatment of the work of labor and nature when expanding the notion of value.

Moreover, the intrinsic value of the 'cheapened' sources of value is defined according to their use-value under capital, whereas the truly intrinsic value can and should be defined outside the realm of capital in the commoning state of living. *The use-value from a non-alienated liveability point of view is essentially different from the use-value achieved under capital.* The latter gains ascendancy over the former facilitated by the surreal world of desires and the capitalist market valuation mechanisms.[14]

The second approach keeps the conceptual scope of capitalist value limited to commodity value. At the level of theoretical abstraction, this method resembles what capital does to nature, that is, reifying or reducing nature to only a background condition necessary for commodity value production. The Marxian version of this approach exposes the mechanisms and consequences of this reduction, which, above all, are the 'metabolic rift' between production and its natural conditions associated with the separation of labor from the natural means and resources of production and a type of alienation from nature due to the dissolution of the 'original unity' between humans, as laboring individuals, and the earth (Saito, 2017b, Saito, 2017a). Accordingly, "the generalised market valuation [of nature] is rooted in the commodification of labour-power based on the separation of the producers from necessary conditions of production, starting with the land" (Burkett, 2006, p. 11).

Nowhere is the opposition between the two camps more starkly exemplified than in debates between Jason W. Moore and Foster–Burkett.[15] Moore criticizes Foster and Burkett for failing to adequately draw on Marx's LTV or to reinterpret it as an ecological value theory. He argues for examining how capitalism has historically developed through nature (a "metabolic shift") rather than simply evolving through creating a "metabolic rift" with nature; a rift, however, that seems rooted in a naive understanding of Marx, one that is afflicted with an epistemological Cartesian dualism, Society" versus "Nature."

Moore's (2015, pp. 147–148) ecological approach to reinterpreting Marxian value theory starts with Marx's arithmetic equation of the (falling) rate of profit. In short, since the organic composition of capital (the ratio of constant capital over variable capital, or c/v) outruns the rate of surplus value or the rate of exploitation (s/v) – due to the constant employment of new technology to increase productivity – the rate of profit, which is $s/(c + v)$, will eventually fall. This tendency is, of course, met with countertendencies mobilized by capital to not only increase the rate of exploitation by intensifying labor but also by cheapening constant capital and variable capital. Capitalism thus relies on cheapening labor power, food, energy, and raw materials, i.e., Moore's "Four Cheaps." Cheaper food, energy, and raw materials help to reduce the value of labor power by reducing the costs of producing means of subsistence, or in other words, reducing the socially necessary labor time needed for labor's reproduction, thus increasing the relative surplus value. Moore sees labor power as part of "Cheap Nature," the "world ecology" of capital. Capital relies vitally on the underpaid work of all Four Cheaps. This way, Moore's approach has the advantage of preventing the dualism of "Society" versus "Nature." His theory aims to show how nature is transformed/produced by capital rather than simply expropriated as a separate entity. Moore argues that the critical analysis of the Capitalocene (a term he uses as an alternative to "Anthropocene") must show "the world-historical process of how humans and nature are incessantly 'co-produced' within the web of life" (Saito, 2017b, p. 281).

Moore's concept of Cheaps broadens the definition of value and surplus value by including the work of extra-human nature. According to Moore, capital exploits whatever can be "capitalized" (paid work/energy) and "appropriates" whatever cannot be immediately capitalized (the "unpaid work/energy of the web of life"). Ecological surplus, as he defines it, is "the ratio"[16] of the former (mass of capital) to the latter (Moore, 2015, pp. 101–102).[17] Capitalist value is entirely reliant on the latter, which should be incorporated into the arithmetic of value theory by expanding fixed and variable capital.

Despite their divergent perspectives, both approaches ultimately result in an unsatisfactory treatment of value. The resulting theories become mere replicas of the capitalist reality, which can be accepted only to the extent that the theory seeks to analyze and critique the system rather than directly transform it. Just as labor is the result of capitalism's primary abstraction of human creativity, the so-called nature is the product of the primary abstraction of the liveability of the life-domain.

Moreover, the Aristotelian taxonomy of value causation can help us better understand the limitations of both opposing perspectives. Those who see the life-domain as a direct source of value (like Jason W. Moore, pre-classical physiocrats, and today's eco-Sraffian energy-value theorists) give primacy to the 'material cause' of value. According to them, the work of labor as part of the life-domain is still crucial as it draws on the riches of the rest of nature, unleashing their surplus-producing capabilities and transforming them into material means of subsistence for humanity. Here, however, value can ultimately be ascribed to objective substances of material condition and subsistence of organized life. Similarly, to consider (the surplus use of) labor power as the primary essence of (surplus) commodity value is to give primacy to the 'efficient cause' of value over the other three types of causation. To consider the "enjoyment of life" or the satisfaction of human needs as the essence of value is to reduce value causation to only a 'final cause' (the subjective and psychological benefits of activities). This theory (as articulated by Daly, Georgescu-Roegen, and Bonaiuti), however, has the advantage of directly attributing normativity to the notion of value – by treating it teleologically as a final cause – but at the cost of sidelining other types of causation.

How can we break through the impasse depicted by the limitations of the two alternative approaches to theorizing the value of so-called 'nature'? As we previously proposed, the answer lies in recognizing four distinct types of value causation and including a normative definition of value in our analyses of capitalist fetish value. The normativity of the former type of value should be based on both the historically actualized and futuristically imagined commoning features of these four types of value causations. *The scope of the analysis should be expanded beyond the inner dynamics of capital to where the decommonization of commoning sources of value occurs.* This is where the bearers of true value are transmuted into the bearers of fetish value. The infra- and meta-processes and meta-mechanisms that underpin these transitions should be the focus of the theory. Since these processes are destabilizing (by destroying the commoning foundations of organized social and ecological life), the civilizing mechanism must also be incorporated into the equation. Moreover, sources and makers of true value are not passive entities subject to capital's 'cannibalism.' The commonizing mechanisms and processes should also be added to the picture; a picture that is more gray than black and white. Does this solution undermine the foundations of the Marxian value theory, or help reconstruct it without violating its underpinning meta-theory?

Abstract labor as the substance of capitalist value does not reflect Marx's normative judgment about value nor even his judgment regarding the primacy of what constitutes value outside capitalist production relations. Indeed, "Marx makes no presumption that the monetary exchange-values of commodities accurately reflect wealth in all its natural and social diversity – either qualitatively or quantitatively" (Burkett, 2006, p. 28). *A critical value theory, to be meaningfully transformative, must be able to show how value in its natural and socially diverse forms* (or at least the use-value of products when determined through unalienating relations*) is lost or expropriated and also show how it can be restored.* If no capitalist value can be assigned to so-called natural wealth, and if a meaningful transition beyond capital requires the (re-)communalization of production and its natural condition, *we are then required to theorize the tensions and interactions between these two types of value: the capitalist/fetish value and the commonist/true value.* This can only be achieved when a more-than-human worldview is adopted in theory and practice that denies the dualism of nature versus humanity. The value of nature cannot be reduced to its use-value when the normativity of use-value is determined through alienating conditions of capital (or any subjugating system).

A comparison of the works of Nancy Fraser and Jason W. Moore can be insightful here. Fraser, too, believes that we need a multi-standard critique of capital. She sees Marx as failing to adequately theorize the abode behind the abode of labor-centered exploitation, that is, the expropriation processes in the spheres of ecology, reproductive labor, and politics. However, Marx showed great interest in these spheres and saw them as entities reduced by capital to only sources of use-value (rather than value) vital to valorization. These spheres are treated by capital as the essential conditions of possibility as far as they are left uncapitalized/un-commodified. To overcome the falling rate of profit, capital keeps expanding its access to these spheres ("accumulation by dispossession" in Harvey's terms). Fraser goes beyond this to articulate Marx's perspective on the extra-labor spheres as background conditions that make it possible for capital to function (Fraser, 2022). She juxtaposes these spheres, but without theorizing how they are interrelated and how they are co-transmuted by becoming empty of their commoning essence while forming a new mechanical totality together (Saito, 2017b, p. 284). The infra-process through which these spheres are turned into conditions of possibility and thus subject to cannibalistic appropriation is what is missing in most (if not all) major theories of capital. This explains why the normative dimension of value remains neglected.

Reducing the extra-labor spheres of value production to passive subjects of appropriation makes it unnecessary for Fraser to reconstruct Marxian value theory by redefining value. Moore, in contrast, recognizes the necessity of theorizing the mutual co-production of capital and the extra-labor (and by extension extra-human) spheres of value production. Yet, this welcome move remains limited to only magnitudes and their ratios/relations under his concept of 'ecological surplus.' Like Fraser, Moore strives to extend the critical theory of capitalism beyond the inner structure of capital. They both build the division between the inner and the outer upon the distinction between 'exploitation' and 'appropriation,' capitalized and uncapitalized. Unlike Fraser, Moore's perspective reduces 'appropriation' to "cheapening," while he applies the term 'exploitation' to encompass not only human labor but also any aspect that can be capitalized upon.

Whether we emphasize the metabolic rift (as in the case of Foster) or the metabolic shift (Moore's argument) in explaining capital's deadly ecological contradictions, the level of analysis needs to go deeper than the 'actual' and extend into the 'real' infra-processes and mechanisms that underpin the co-devolution of all the spheres of value production into the mechanically entangled conditions of possibility for capital. Each one of these spheres in our multi-standard critique of capital plays the role of a different type of causality in causing value. We can then incorporate them into our account of value without violating Marx's emphasis on commodified labor power as the source of surplus value. Our theory maintains a central focus on production without descending into productivism.

Notes

1 The implications of advancements in late capitalist production relations for the Marxian LTV have been debated among post-Marxists and Marxist revisionists, and between the two camps. These advancements are identified under different titles. Some highlight new episodes in the history of capitalism that differ from the time when Marx developed his value theory, others emphasize new processes that challenge the validity of LTV: deindustrialization, the precarization of labor, socialization of production, Industry 4.0, etc.

2 These theories have been criticized for their Eurocentric focus, as they tend to represent the middle classes while excluding the lived experiences of workers in poorer communities. This criticism may not necessarily question their explanatory power in relevant contexts where late capitalism is expanding through new technologies. This trend includes many growing sectors in the global South as well, where the boundaries between social production and social reproduction have been collapsing due to factors such as the gig economy, deindustrialization (Benanav, 2020), precariatization, and political and legal institutions that are unable to curtail the cruel and naked political power of capital.

3 There are authors who see Negri and Marx complementing each other. Tremčinský (2022) uses the example of a machine harvesting body energy out of a resting person to mine cryptocurrency to illustrate how digital capitalism extracts value from social reproduction processes. Tremčinský argues that the decentralization of socialized production does not however make the Marxian value theory obsolete. Rather, "the capitalist command of labour can be directly incorporated into the design of these structures and serve to extract value" (2022, p. 20). Being politically decentralized, Bitcoin shows that control via economic appropriation and ownership can still be the prominent form of power under capital that capitalizes on socialized work. Bitcoin can thus serve as an exemplar of an emerging relation of production where the decentralized autonomous networks are designed to extract surplus value without necessarily resorting to the centralized political command" (Tremčinský, 2022, p. 32).

4 If wage labor is not the sole source of capitalist value, then it is necessary to broaden our understanding of how such value is extracted and manufactured in fetishistic forms through mechanisms that may differ from those found within the workplace.

5 "The New Interpretation makes the following claims regarding the labour theory of value. First, all value-added derives from the expenditure of direct living labour. Second, values are measured in hours of abstract labour time and prices are measured in monetary units. Third, the value of the output is determined by the sum of the values of the non-labour inputs used up (labelled past or indirect labour) and the direct labour time spent. The non-labour inputs transfer their value to the output, while direct living labour creates new value-added … Surplus value (the value corresponding to unpaid labour time) is the origin of aggregate profits. Hence, the rate of exploitation measures surplus value divided by the value of labour power or, equivalently, unpaid over paid labour time" (Rotta and Paraná, 2022, p. 1050).

6 Value-added (VA) is defined as the sum of variable capital and surplus value ($v + s$). It is argued that only living labor (in total L) that adds value to the inputs of production. Therefore, VA is proportional to the total labor expended, aL or the difference between c' and c.

7 Rigi (2014, 2015) believes that since Marx's theory of value differentiates between value and price, and since it is possible to have profit without producing value, products produced without expending labor time do not 'add' value even if they generate revenue. Therefore, LTV cannot be refuted on the basis that such products convey value without having labor time contained in them. Parkhurst (2019) argues that Rigi fails to prove that DI production, by its very nature, is non-value productive. However, he does not attempt to show that some, if not all, DI is value productive.

8 Marx excludes the labor time expended in the original production of a commodity and instead emphasizes the most recent cycles of its re/production for the estimation of its socially necessary labor time or the abstract value contained. Therefore, following Marx, it is argued that as the share of labor time in the reproduction of immaterial commodities (such as digital information) approaches a negligible amount, LTV can no longer explain exploitation. However, critics of this argue that what is perceived as the so-called reproduction of immaterial commodities (such as the transfer of the digital replica of a software program to the computer of a buyer) should be regarded as an act of distribution rather than reproduction (Parkhurst, 2019, p. 81). Moreover, as Parkhurst (2019, p. 84) reminds us, "[i]narguably, capitalist firms that produce DI sometimes receive more profit than corresponds to amount of surplus labour they preside over. … But there is nothing novel or paradigm-shifting about this. Superprofits can be secured by any highly efficient or monopolistic firm, irrespective of whether its products are immaterial or instead fully corporeal and tangible."

9 Capital has an inherent inclination toward maximizing profit, resulting in excess investment and overproduction, and thus paradoxically a decline in their profitability and "a system-wide evening-out of the rate of return on investment" (Parkhurst, 2019, p. 73).

10 See Keen (2021) for a further discussion of the problem of externalities.

11 Attribution of terms like 'techno-feudalism' as the endpoint to capitalism follows a technologically deterministic logic that can mislead liberation praxis by propagating a delusion that any coordinated action against oligarchic technocracies (like boycotting Amazon) can contribute to some sort of liberation. The emergence of these concepts in the literature, however, indicates a need for renewing the emphasis on the political or power-coercive aspect of exploitation, as opposed to pure 'economic means' of coercion or social control.

12 If the wage or basic income is supposed to be paid by the state out of its revenue, it will help capital by transferring the responsibility to the state (as another social institution alongside the household). This would be the transfer of the treatment of socio-economic costs of the social reproduction of labor, as a social externality, from the domestic sphere to the public sphere.

13 As Burkett (2006, pp. 16–17) discusses, Marx did not criticize physiocrats for attributing use-value to nature. Rather, he criticized them for conflating capitalist exchange-value with its natural basis.

14 The greening of Marxist theory, which seeks to conflate the value of the work of nature with that of labor, is confronted with the challenge of translating the value of nature into prices, just as the classical LTV struggled with the transformation problem.

15 Nevertheless, both sides agree that Marx's ecological perspective exists.

16 Here, Moore appears to conflate the rate of exploitation with surplus by using the term 'ratio' instead of 'difference.'

17 For Moore, capital is therefore more than an abstract movement of value. To prevent the fall of the ecological surplus, capital must actively draw on expanding the unpaid reproductive work of both human and extra-human natures. However, the Four Cheaps (or the Seven Cheaps in his later work) finally cease being cheap, and thus, the ecological surplus falls.

Epilogue

This first edition of our short book remains a work in progress. It is an invitation to engage in a new and hopefully productive dialogue on how to address the challenges of understanding the intricate relationship between value and capital. We believe our proposed approach has also the potential to impact post-capitalist transformative theory and revolutionary praxis. We posit that 'value' must be re-examined and liberated from its subservient ties to capital. However, this must not come at the expense of disregarding how capital appropriates value. Under capitalism, value loses its inherent normativity, and Marxist critics have not provided a positive normative framework for capital as 'value' in motion. This conceptual ambiguity has led to confusion and division among critical theorists.

On one hand, some argue that the notion of value should encompass all inputs involved in capitalist value production while conflating intrinsic value and commodity value. On the other hand, others warn about this conflation, viewing it as an erroneous attempt to treat capital as a transhistorical phenomenon. Capital appropriates intrinsic value and transforms it into its own version of value, the commodity or capitalist value, while fetishizing it. The antipode should be to defetishize value by rejecting the commonly accepted idea of its objectivity.

Marx's distinctions between abstract and concrete labor, use-value, and exchange-value, enabled him to expose certain erroneous assumptions of bourgeois political economy. However, it would be inconsistent for critical theory to overlook the differentiation between *true value* and *fetish value* as two interconnected ideal–typical constructs. We view (true) 'value' as the antithesis of capital, demonstrating how capital drains our world of (true) value. This is the pivotal step in the process of *defetishizing fetish value*, which has become omnipresent; the definitive source of worldwide devastation, subjugation, and injustice, yet entrenched to reveal its fundamental anti-normative nature.

Merely redefining the concept of value is insufficient however without establishing the foundations for new value regimes relevant to the creation of genuine value. For care, love, justice, autonomy, social and ecological well-being, conviviality, and cooperation to flourish as 'sustainable sources' of authentic (true) value, they must be integrated into *a commonist way of life* – a paradigmatically distinct value regime from that of capitalist value extraction.

Typically, most individuals engage in activities that enhance their lives and those of others, creating true value. However, some actively participate in a spectrum of social struggles to resist capitalism and reclaim what has been lost to its power. Whether through direct confrontation or civil disobedience, these efforts generate true value as they draw upon *commoning praxes* and *surviving commons*. Some struggles may even succeed in preserving and reclaiming parts of the commons from the encroachment of capital. Others endeavor to create commons-like ecosystems and expand them, establishing worker-owned cooperatives, social solidarity economies, community wealth-building initiatives, regenerative systems of food production, time banks, community gardens, peer-to-peer production, and sharing economies. These struggles have enabled us to create conditions of possibility for generating (true) value.

However, we must acknowledge the reality that we are all passengers on a train propelled by capital, hurtling toward a cliff at an increasingly rapid pace. While some of the value produced may alleviate hardships of life and even slow the unfolding catastrophes in certain places, it is imperative to recognize that these efforts are occurring within the confines of the train and, so far, have had little impact on its trajectory. Exiting the train is a costly endeavor and not a viable option for many. The train is peculiar in that it drags its external environment towards the precipice along with it. While it may be necessary to uncouple a few carriages or negotiate with those in the first-class section or with the train drivers (the states) to secure a more equitable distribution of welfare or social protection or to engage in political action to delay the onset of disasters, such measures are at best short-term and only partial solutions. They may even divert attention away from addressing the root causes of the crisis and finding necessary radical and sustainable solutions.

Political revolutions aiming to take control of the train are becoming increasingly necessary. However, the history of the past century demonstrates that even the most remarkable revolutions cannot guarantee salvation. We must avoid seeing any solution as exclusively immune to corruption. Even well-crafted strategies, if they do not prioritize a paradigm shift, risk falling into the hands of those who hold power and prioritize the extraction value.

What fuels the train of 'civilization' is value. Value is what societies hold dear and strive towards realizing in any objective form possible. Drawing on thermodynamic terminology, metaphorically speaking, true value is akin to free energy that can be captured and transformed to promote the self-regeneration and expansion of life, while fetish value is like waste heat that dissipates without being of genuine use and entails significant harm.

Life is in a constant battle against entropy. Life harnesses the free energy distributed due to entropy and transforms it into forms necessary for its own regeneration and expansion. This is achieved through the labor of living organisms, which possess the creative power to do so. This is how life functions creatively. True value is the product of this perennial struggle, which manifests in social and ecological graces such as good health, a thriving society, and a fulfilling life. Individual organisms borrow true value from the larger system to flourish and self-actualize. They, in turn, produce true value to inject back into the system and allow others to thrive. This is the miraculous circle of life.

Life resists the effects of entropy by organizing itself in diverse commons-based forms of social and ecological cooperation. From the earliest forms of life to complex organisms and entire ecosystems, commoning has been and remains a key strategy for overcoming the challenges of thermodynamic decay. Just as life harnesses the power of entropy to create, regenerate, and sustain itself, capital embodies the inverse force, constantly expropriating and eroding the foundations of life in its endless and aggressive quest for profit and growth.

As we conclude this epilogue to the open-ended dialogue we started in this book, let us embrace the urgency of the radical paradigm shift required to challenge the destructive forces of capital. Let us reclaim value from its grasp and forge a future that transcends the contradictions of capitalism by redefining the very essence of value, with the aim of creating new societies that nurture the flourishing and liberation of all.

References

Al-Amoudi, I. (2022). Are post-human technologies dehumanizing? Human enhancement and artificial intelligence in contemporary societies. *Journal of Critical Realism, 21*(5), 516–538.

Albritton, R. *et al.* (2004). *New socialisms: Futures beyond globalization.* London: Routledge.

Allen, G. E. (2017). Mechanism, organism, and vitalism. In S. Glennan & P. M. Illari (Eds.), *The Routledge handbook of mechanisms and mechanical philosophy* (pp. 59–73). London and New York: Routledge.

Archer, M. S. (2015). *Generative mechanisms transforming the social order.* Cham: Springer.

Armstrong McKay, D. I., *et al.* (2022). Exceeding 1.5°C global warming could trigger multiple climate tipping points. *Science, 377*(6611), eabn7950.

Arvidsson, A., & Colleoni, E. (2012). Value in informational capitalism and on the Internet. *Information Society, 28*(3), 135–150.

Azzellini, D. (2016). Labour as a commons: The example of worker-recuperated companies. *Critical Sociology, 44*(4–5), 763–776.

Banfield, G. (2015). *Critical realist for Marxist sociology of education.* London: Routledge.

Basso, L. (2015). *Marx and the common: From capital to the late writings.* Leiden and Boston: Brill.

Bellofiore, R. (2018). Forever young? Marx's critique of political economy after 200 years. *PSL Quarterly Review, 71*(287), 353–388.

Bellofiore, R., & Coveri, A. (2022). The transformation problem. In B. Skeggs *et al.* (Eds.), *The Sage handbook of Marxism* (1st ed., pp. 171–187). Los Angeles, CA: Sage.

Benanav, A. (2020). *Automation and the future of work.* London and New York: Verso.

Bhaskar, R. (1986). *Scientific realism and human emancipation.* London: Verso.

Bhaskar, R. (2018). *Empiricism and the metatheory of the social sciences.* London and New York: Routledge.

Bhaskar, R., & Callinicos, A. (2003). Marxism and critical realism: A debate. *Journal of Critical Realism, 1*(2), 89–114.

Bhattacharya, T. (2017). *Social reproduction theory: Remapping class, recentring oppression.* London: Pluto Press.

Blackledge, P. (2015). G.A. Cohen and the limits of analytical Marxism. In M. J. Thompson (Ed.), *Constructing Marxist ethics: Critique, normativity, praxis* (pp. 288–312). Leiden and Boston: Brill.

Buckley, W. F. (1967). *Sociology and modern systems theory.* Englewood Cliffs, NJ: Prentice-Hall.

Burkett, P. (2006). *Marxism and ecological economics: Toward a red and green political economy*. Leiden and Boston: Brill.

Byrd, D. J. (2019). Ali Shariati (1933–1977). In I. Ness & Z. Cope (Eds.), *The Palgrave encyclopedia of imperialism and anti-imperialism* (pp. 1–16). Cham: Springer International Publishing.

Celikates, R., & Jaeggi, R. (2017). Technology and reification: "Technology and science as 'ideology'" (1968). In B. Hauke *et al.* (Eds.), *The Habermas handbook* (pp. 256–270). New York, Chichester, and West Sussex: Columbia University Press.

Chagnon, C. W., Durante, F., Gills, B. K., Hagolani-Albov, S. E., Hokkanen, S., Kangasluoma, S. M. J., … Vuola, M. P. S. (2022). From extractivism to global extractivism: The evolution of an organizing concept. *Journal of Peasant Studies*, *49*(4), 760–792.

Chomsky, N., & Prashad, V. (2022). *The withdrawal: Iraq, Libya, Afghanistan, and the fragility of U.S. power*. New York: The New Press.

Christophers, B. (2016). Risking value theory in the political economy of finance and nature. *Progress in Human Geography*, *42*(3), 330–349.

Cogliano, J. F. (2018). Surplus value production and realization in Marxian theory - Applications to the U.S., 1990–2015. *Review of Political Economy*, *30*(4), 505–533.

Davies, W. (2015). *The happiness industry: How the government and big business sold us well-being*. London: Verso.

Dean, J. (2020). Communism or neo-feudalism? *New Political Science*, *42*(1), 1–17.

De Angelis, M. (1995). Beyond the technological and the social paradigms: A political reading of abstract labour as the substance of value. *Capital and Class*, *57*(57), 107–134.

De Angelis, M. (2007). *The beginning of history: Value struggles and global capital*. London: Pluto Press.

De Angelis, M. (2022). Commons. In B. Skeggs *et al.* (Eds.), *The sage handbook of Marxism* (1st ed., pp. 643–661). Los Angeles, CA: Sage.

de Beauvoir, S. (2015). *The ethics of ambiguity*. New York: Philosophical Library.

Demichelis, L., & Caution, L. (2022). *Marx, alienation and techno-capitalism*. Basingstoke: Palgrave Macmillan.

Desai, R. (2020). Marx's critical political economy, Marxist economics and actually occurring revolutions against capitalism. *Third World Quarterly*, *41*(8), 1353–1370.

Desai, R. (2023). *Capitalism, coronavirus and war: A geopolitical economy*. Abingdon, Oxon, and New York: Routledge.

Dobb, M. (1972). *Political economy and capitalism: Some essays in economic tradition*. Westport, CT: Greenwood Press.

Eagleton, T. (2011). *Why Marx was right*. New Haven, CT: Yale University Press.

Elson, D. (1979). The value theory of labour. In D. Elson (Ed.), *Value: The representation of labour in capitalism* (pp. 115–118). London: Verso.

Engels, F. (1947). *Anti-Dühring: Herr Eugen Dühring's revolution in science*. Moscow: Progress Publishers.

Federici, S. (2019). *Re-enchanting the world: Feminism and the politics of the commons*. Oakland, CA: PM Press.

Fleetwood, S. (2002). What kind of theory is Marx's labour theory of value? In S. Fleetwood *et al.* (Eds.), *Critical realism and Marxism* (pp. 57–87). New York: Routledge.

Fortunati, L., & Fleming, J. (1995). *The arcane of reproduction: Housework, prostitution, labor and capital*. New York: Autonomedia.

Foster, J. B. (2022). *Capitalism in the Anthropocene: Ecological ruin or ecological revolution.* New York: Monthly Review Press.

Foster, J. B., & Burkett, P. (2016). *Marx and the earth: An anti-critique.* Historical Materialism Book Series. Leiden and Boston: Brill, x, 316 pages.

Foster, J. B., & Burkett, P. (2018). Value isn't everything. *Monthly Review, 70*(6), 1–17.

Foster, J. B., & Clark, B. (2020). *The robbery of nature: Capitalism and the ecological rift.* New York: Monthly Review Press.

Foster, J. B. *et al.* (2010). *The ecological rift: Capitalism's war on the earth.* New York: Monthly Review Press.

Fraser, N. (2014). Behind Marx's hidden abode: For an expanded conception of capitalism. *New Left Review, 86*(86), 55–72.

Fraser, N. (2022). *Cannibal capitalism: How our system is devouring democracy, care, and the planet and what we can do about It.* London and New York: Verso.

Fuchs, C. (2010). Labor in informational capitalism and on the Internet. *Information Society, 26*(3), 179–196.

Fuchs, C., & Mosco, V. (2016). *Marx in the age of digital capitalism.* Leiden and Boston: Brill.

Gibson-Graham, J. K. (1996). *The end of capitalism (as we knew it): A feminist critique of political economy.* Cambridge, MA and Oxford: Blackwell Publishers.

Gibson, K., *et al.* (2015). *Manifesto for living in the Anthropocene.* London: Punctum Books.

Gills, B. K., & Hosseini, S. A. H. (2022). Pluriversality and beyond: Consolidating radical alternatives to (mal-)development as a Commonist project. *Sustainability Science, 17*(4), 1183–1194.

Gimenez, M. (2018). *Marx, women, and capitalist social reproduction: Marxist feminist essays.* Boston: Brill.

Gorz, A. (1999). *Reclaiming work: Beyond the wage-based society.* Cambridge: Polity.

Graeber, D. (2001). *Toward an anthropological theory of value: The false coin of our own dreams.* New York: Palgrave.

Graeber, D. (2013). It is value that brings universes into being. *HAU: Journal of Ethnographic Theory, 3*(2), 219–243.

Gray, K., & Gills, B. K. (2022). Post-covid transformations. In *Rethinking globalizations* (1st ed.). London: Routledge.

Gross, N. (2009). A pragmatist theory of social mechanisms. *American Sociological Review, 74*(3), 358–379.

Hardt, M., & Negri, A. (2004). *Multitude: War and democracy in the age of Empire.* New York: The Penguin Press.

Hardt, M., & Negri, A. (2009). *Commonwealth.* Cambridge, MA: Belknap Press of Harvard University Press.

Harré, R., & Madden, E. H. (1975). *Causal powers: A theory of natural necessity.* Oxford: Blackwell.

Harvey, D. (2003). *The new imperialism.* Oxford and New York: Oxford University Press.

Harvey, D. (2004). The 'new' imperialism: Accumulation by dispossession. *Socialist Register, 40*, 63–87.

Harvey, D. (2014). *Seventeen contradictions and the end of capitalism.* London: Profile Books.

Harvey, D. (2018a). Marx's refusal of the labor theory of value. *https://davidharvey. org/2018/03/marxs-refusal-of-the-labour-theory-of-value-by-david-harvey/.*

Harvey, D. (2018b). *Marx, capital and the madness of economic reason*. New York: Oxford University Press.

Heinrich, M. (2021). *How to read Marx's capital: Commentary and explanations on the beginning chapters*. New York: Monthly Review Press.

Hosseini, S. A. H. (2011). *Alternative globalizations: An integrative approach to studying dissident knowledge in the global justice movement*. Milton Park and New York: Routledge.

Hosseini, S. A. H. (2013). Occupy cosmopolitanism: Ideological Transversalization in the age of global economic uncertainties. *Globalizations, 10*(3), 425–438.

Hosseini, S. A. H. (2015). Transversality in diversity: Experiencing networks of confusion and convergence in the world social forum. *International and Multidisciplinary Journal of Social Sciences-RIMCIS, 4*(1), 54–87.

Hosseini, S. A. H. (2018a). From commoning the alternatives to Commonism as an integral alternative to capitalism. In S. A. H. Hosseini (Ed.), *Alternative Futures and Regional Prospects Symposium*. UTS, Sydney: University of Newcastle, Australia.

Hosseini, S. A. H. (2018b). From well-being to well-living: Towards a post-capitalist understanding of quality of life. *AQ - Australian Quarterly, 89*(2), 35–39.

Hosseini, S. A. H. (2020). On the urgency of (Re)integrating with the radical. *Global Dialogue: Magazine of the International Sociological Association, 10*. Retrieved November 10, 2020, from.

Hosseini, S. A. H. (2021). The paradoxical nature of well-being under capitalism: A glimpse from the Sem analysis of the 2012 Australian world values survey data into the social determinants of subjective well-being, *Advance*, Preprint (pp. 1–4). https://doi.org/10.31124/advance.13269389.v2

Hosseini, S. A. H. (2022a). Capital as 'fetish value' has no 'true value': Beyond the divide between the analytical and the normative. *SocArXiv*. https://doi.org/10.31235/osf.io/vahny.

Hosseini, S. A. H. (2022b). Labor redefined: Toward a Commonist value theory of labor under and beyond capital. *SocArXiv*. https://doi.org/10.31235/osf.io/ev2m3.

Hosseini, S. A. H., & Gills, B. K. (2020a). Beyond the critical: Reinventing the radical imagination in transformative development and global(ization) studies. *Globalizations, 17*(8), 1350–1366.

Hosseini, S. A. H., & Gills, B. K. (2020b). Reinventing global studies through transformative scholarship: A critical proposition. In S. A. H. Hosseini *et al.* (Eds.), *The Routledge handbook of transformative global studies* (pp. 13–28). London: Routledge.

Hosseini, S. A. H. *et al.* (2020). Towards new agendas for transformative global studies: An introduction. In S. A. H. Hosseini *et al.* (Eds.), *The Routledge handbook of transformative global studies* (pp. 1–10). London: Routledge.

Hosseini, S. A. H. *et al.* (2022). Right-wing populism in a global perspective: The necessity for an integrative theory. In R. Baikady *et al.* (Eds.), *The Palgrave handbook of global social change* (pp.1–24). Cham: Springer International Publishing.

Hudis, P. (2019). Marx's concept of socialism. In M. Vidal *et al.* (Eds.), *The Oxford handbook of Karl Marx* (pp. 757–772). Oxford: Oxford University Press.

Hudson, M. (2015). *Killing the host: How financial parasites and debt bondage destroy the global economy*. Petrolia; CA: Counterpunch Books.

Kay, J. (2007). *The arcane of reproductive production*. Retrieved February 3, 2023, from https://libcom.org/library/aufheben/aufheben-13-2005/the-arcane-of-reproductive-production.

Keen, S. (2021). The appallingly bad neoclassical economics of climate change. *Globalizations, 18*(7), 1149–1177.

Kieve, R. A. (1983). The Hegelian inversion: On the possibility of a Marxist dialectic. *Science and Society, 47*(1), 37–65.

Kockelman, P. (2015). Four theories of things: Aristotle, Marx, Heidegger, and Peirce. *Signs and Society, 3*(1), 153–192.

Krotz, F. (2007). The meta-process of 'mediatization' as a conceptual frame. *Global Media and Communication, 3*(3), 256–260.

Kurki, M. (2008). *Causation in international relations: Reclaiming causal analysis.* Cambridge and New York: Cambridge University Press.

Kurki, M. (2020). *International relations in a relational universe.* Oxford: Oxford University Press.

Levine, N. (2021). *Marx's resurrection of Aristotle.* Basingstoke: Palgrave Macmillan.

Marsden, R. (1999). *The nature of capital: Marx after Foucault.* London: Routledge.

Marx, K. (1973). *Grundrisse: Foundations of the critique of political economy.* London: Allen Lane; New Left Review.

Marx, K. (1989). Marginal notes on Adolph Wagner's Lehrbuch der politischen Ökonomie. In J Cohen, et al. *Marx-Engels collected works* (Vol. 24, pp. 531–562). New York: International Publishers.

Marx, K. (1990). *Capital: A critique of political economy, volume I.* London: Penguin Books in Association with New Left Review.

Marx, K. (1993). *Grundrisse: Foundations of the critique of political economy (rough draft).* London and New York: Penguin Books in association with New Left Review.

Marx, K. (2001). *Capital: Volume III.* London: Electric Book Co.

Marx, K., & Engels, F. (1998). *The German ideology: Including theses on Feuerbach and introduction to the critique of political economy.* Amherst, NY: Prometheus Books.

Marx, K., & Engels, F. (2002). *The communist manifesto.* London: Penguin.

Marx, K., & Krader, L. (1974). *The ethnological notebooks of Karl Marx: (Studies of Morgan, Phear, Maine, Lubbock).* Assen: Van Gorcum.

Marx, K. et al. (1988). *Economic and philosophic manuscripts of 1844.* Buffalo, NY: Prometheus Books.

Mau, S. (2022). The body. In B. Skeggs et al. (Eds.), *The Sage handbook of Marxism* (1st ed., pp. 1268–1286). Los Angeles, CA: Sage.

Mazzucato, M. (2018). *The value of everything: Making and taking in the global economy.* London: Allen Lane.

McCarthy, G. E. (1990). *Marx and the ancients: Classical ethics, social justice, and nineteenth-century political economy.* Savage, MD: Rowman & Littlefield.

McCarthy, J. (2005). Commons as counterhegemonic projects. *Capitalism, Nature, Socialism, 16*(1), 9–24.

Meadows, D. H., & Club of Rome (1972). *The limits to growth: A report for the Club of Rome's project on the predicament of mankind.* London: Earth Island.

Meadows, D. H. et al. (2004). *The limits to growth: The 30-year update.* White River Junction, VT: Chelsea Green Publishing Company.

Mella Méndez, L., & Carby-Hall, J. (2020). *Labour law and the gig economy: Challenges posed by the digitalisation of labour processes.* London: Routledge.

Mies, M. (1986). *Patriarchy and accumulation on a world scale: Women in the international division of labour.* London: Zed Books.

Moore, J. W. (2015). *Capitalism in the web of life: Ecology and the accumulation of capital.* New York: Verso.

Moore, J. W. (2017a). The Capitalocene, Part I: On the nature and origins of our ecological crisis. *Journal of Peasant Studies*, *44*(3), 594–630.

Moore, J. W. (2017b). Metabolic rift or metabolic shift? Dialectics, nature, and the world-historical method. *Theory and Society*, *46*(4), 285–318.

Moore, J. W. (2018). The Capitalocene Part II: Accumulation by appropriation and the centrality of unpaid work/energy. *Journal of Peasant Studies*, *45*(2), 237–279.

Mukumbang, F. C. (2021). Retroductive theorizing: A contribution of critical realism to mixed methods research. *Journal of Mixed Methods Research*, *14*(1), 93–114.

Negri, A. (1988). *Revolution retrieved: Writings on Marx, Keynes, capitalist crisis, and new social subjects (1967–83)*. London: Red [Notes].

Negri, A., & Emery, E. (2018). *From the factory to the metropolis*. Cambridge and Malden, MA: Polity Press.

Ostrom, E. (2015). *Governing the commons: The evolution of institutions for collective action*. Cambridge: Cambridge University Press.

Ouellet, M. (2015). Revisiting Marx's value theory: Elements of a critical theory of immaterial labor in information capitalism. *Information Society*, *31*(1), 20–27.

Panayotakis, C. *et al.* (2021). *The capitalist mode of destruction: Austerity, ecological crisis and the hollowing out of democracy*. Manchester: Manchester University Press.

Parkhurst, B. (2019). Digital information and value: A response to Jakob Rigi. *TripleC*, *17*(1), 72–85.

Patel, R., & Moore, J. W. (2018). *A history of the world in seven cheap things: A guide to capitalism, nature, and the future of the planet*. London: Verso.

Peneder, M. (2009). The meaning of entrepreneurship: A modular concept. *Journal of Industry, Competition and Trade*, *9*(2), 77–99.

Piketty, T., & Goldhammer, A. (2020). *Capital and ideology*. Cambridge: The Belknap Press of Harvard University Press.

Pisters, P., & Braidotti, R. (2012). *Revisiting normativity with Deleuze*. London: Bloomsbury Publishing.

Pitts, F. H. (2021). *Value*. Cambridge and Medford, MA: Polity Press.

Pomeroy, A. F. (2004). *Marx and whitehead: Process, dialectics, and the critique of capitalism*. Albany, NY: State University of New York Press.

Pratten, S. (2009). Critical realism and causality: Tracing the Aristotelian legacy. *Journal for the Theory of Social Behaviour*, *39*(2), 189–218.

Rahnema, A. (2008). Ali Shariati: Teacher, preacher, rebel. In A. Rahnema (Ed.), *Pioneers of Islamic revival* (pp. 208–250). New York: Zed Books.

Rigi, J. (2014). Foundations of a Marxist theory of the political economy of information: Trade secrets and intellectual property, and the production of relative surplus value and the extraction of rent-tribute. *TripleC*, *12*(2), 909–936.

Rigi, J. (2015). The demise of the Marxian law of value? A critique of Michael Hardt and Antonio Negri. In E. Fisher & C. Fuchs (Eds.), *Reconsidering value and labour in the digital age* (pp.188–206). New York: Palgrave Macmillan.

Rigi, J., & Prey, R. (2015). Value, rent, and the political economy of social media. *Information Society*, *31*(5), 392–406.

Riva, T. R. (2022). Value. In B. Skeggs *et al.* (Eds.), *The sage handbook of Marxism* (1st ed., pp. 85–101). Los Angeles, CA: Sage.

Rodríguez-Rocha, V. (2021). Social reproduction theory: State of the field and new directions in geography. *Geography Compass*, *15*(8), 1–16.

Rotta, T. N., & Paraná, E. (2022). Bitcoin as a digital commodity. *New Political Economy*, *27*(6), 1046–1061.

Saito, K. (2017a). *Karl Marx's ecosocialism: Capitalism, nature, and the unfinished critique of political economy.* New York: Monthly Review Press.

Saito, K. (2017b). Marx in the Anthropocene: Value, metabolic rift, and the non-Cartesian dualism. *Zeitschrift fuer Kritische Sozialtheorie und Philosophie, 4*(1–2), 276–295.

Schilling, M. A. (2000). Toward a general modular systems theory and its application to interfirm product modularity. *Academy of Management Review, 25*(2), 312–334.

Sevilla-Buitrago, A. (2015). Capitalist formations of enclosure: Space and the extinction of the commons. *Antipode, 47*(4), 999–1020.

Sharī'atī '. (1976). *BāZgasht [return to the self].* Tihrān: Ḥusaynīyah-i Irshād.

Sinclair, M. (2017). *The actual and the possible: Modality and metaphysics in modern philosophy.* Oxford: Oxford University Press.

Smetona, M. J. (2015). Marx's normative understanding of the capitalist system. *Rethinking Marxism, 27*(1), 51–64.

Smith, J. E. (2022). Automation. In B. Skeggs *et al.* (Eds.), *The sage handbook of Marxism* (1st ed., pp. 135–152). Los Angeles, CA: Sage.

Starosta, G. (2022). Labour. In B. Skeggs *et al.* (Eds.), *The sage handbook of Marxism* (1st ed., pp. 118–134). Los Angeles, CA: Sage.

Staveren IV. (2001). *The values of economics: An Aristotelian perspective.* London and New York: Routledge.

Thatcher, J., O'Sullivan, D., & Mahmoudi, D. (2016). Data colonialism through accumulation by dispossession: New metaphors for daily data. *Environment and Planning. Part D, 34*(6), 990–1006.

Tombazos, S. (2020). Capital as 'abstraction in action' and economic rhythms in Marx. *Cambridge Journal of Economics, 44*(5), 1055–1068.

Tremčinský, M. (2022). Labour, control, and value: Marx Meets Negri in bitcoin mining. *Dialectical Anthropology, 46*(1), 17–34.

Vandenberghe, F. (2019). The normative foundations of critical realism: A comment on Dave Elder-Vass and Leigh Price. *Journal of Critical Realism, 18*(3), 319–336.

Varoufakis, Y. (2021). *Techno-feudalism is taking over.* Retrieved June 28, 2021, from https://www.proiect-svndicate.org/commentarv/technofeudalism-replacing-market -capitalism-bv-vanis-varoufakis-2021-06.16.4.2022.

Vitale, S. (2020). Beyond "homo laborans": Marx's dialectical account of human essence. *Social Theory and Practice, 46*(3), 633–655.

Vogel, L. (1983). *Marxism and the oppression of women: Toward a unitary theory.* New Brunswick, NJ: Rutgers University Press.

Wajcman, J. (2022). Automation: Is it really different this time? A summary review. In F. Butollo *et al.* (Eds.), *Marx and the robots: Networked production, AI and human labour* (pp. 10–21). London: Pluto Press.

Wark, M. (2019). *Capital is dead.* London and New York: Verso.

Weeks, K. (2011). *The problem with work: Feminism, Marxism, antiwork politics, and postwork imaginaries.* Durham, NC: Duke University Press.

Wimmer, C. (2020). The automatic revolution. *Capital and Class, 44*(2), 287–292.

Wright, E. O. (1994). *Interrogating inequality: Essays on class analysis, socialism and Marxism.* London: Verso.

Ylikoski, P. (2017). Social mechanisms. In S. Glennan & P. M. Illari (Eds.), *The Routledge handbook of mechanisms and mechanical philosophy* (pp. 401–412). London and New York: Routledge.

Zakrzewski, A. *et al.* (2022). Standing Still Is Not an Option: Global Wealth 2022, Boston Consulting Group, Boston, https://web-assets.bcg.com/24/f5/ f3776eb4427fa57471dddc921211/bcg-global-wealth-standing-still-is-not-an-option-jun-2022-r-4.pdf.

Index

For Product Safety Concerns and Information please contact our EU
representative GPSR@taylorandfrancis.com
Taylor & Francis Verlag GmbH, Kaufingerstraße 24, 80331 München, Germany